19TH CENTURY BARNSLEY MURDERS

19TH CENTURY BARNSLEY MURDERS

MARGARET DRINKALL

PEN & SWORD
TRUE CRIME

First published in Great Britain in 2015 by
Pen & Sword True Crime
an imprint of
Pen & Sword Books Ltd
47 Church Street
Barnsley
South Yorkshire
S70 2AS

ISBN 978 1 47382 735 6

A CIP catalogue record for this book is available from the British
Library.

Typeset in Plantin by
Mac Style Ltd, Bridlington, East Yorkshire
Printed and bound in the UK by CPI Group (UK) Ltd, Croydon,
CR0 4YY

Pen & Sword Books Ltd incorporates the imprints of Pen &
Sword Archaeology, Atlas, Aviation, Battleground, Discovery,
Family History, History, Maritime, Military, Naval, Politics,
Railways, Select, Transport, True Crime, and Fiction, Frontline
Books, Leo Cooper, Praetorian Press, Seaforth Publishing and
Wharncliffe.

For a complete list of Pen & Sword titles please contact
PEN & SWORD BOOKS LIMITED
47 Church Street, Barnsley, South Yorkshire S70 2AS, England
E-mail: enquiries@pen-and-sword.co.uk
Website: www.pen-and-sword.co.uk

Contents

Acknowledgements

Writing a book is always teamwork and I would like to thank Roni Wilkinson from Pen and Sword Books for his encouragement. I would also like to thank Matt Jones for his help with the production of the book, Linne Matthews for her skilful editing, and Mat Blurton for the book design. I have also had occasion to pick the brains of retired Detective Constable Philip Howling, who has been unfailing in offering advice about police and legal matters, for which I am truly grateful. I would also like to thank the staff of the Barnsley Archives and Local Studies department for permission to print several old photographs from their collection.

Last, but never least, my son Chris, whose expert knowledge of IT systems and photography I would be lost without.

Introduction

The town of Barnsley has great historical significance. It was first mentioned in the Domesday Book, where it was referred to as Berneslai. Barnsley originally developed as a centre for linen weaving, a trade that attracted many artisans to the town. The downside to industrial growth and rapid urbanization resulted in the development of slums, which spread as more and more people flooded in. Where there are slums it is almost inevitable that crime will flourish. But the boom was not to last and soon the cotton districts of Yorkshire overtook the linen trade, leaving behind chronic unemployment and terrible living conditions. Modern-day Barnsley still shows signs of having lost the glory it enjoyed in the nineteenth century, when it was recognized as an important manufacturing town.

Thankfully, coal mining was another staple industry for the area, and the rich Barnsley seam provided work for many. This was one of the most important coal seams in the country during the nineteenth century, which produced 50 per cent of the whole output for South Yorkshire. With the introduction of canals such as the Dearne and Dove to transport the coal, miners came to the area seeking work. With the mining of a rich seam of coal, accidents were bound to happen. On 19 February 1857, it was reported that 189 men and boys were buried alive at Lundhill Colliery following a heavy underground explosion. Sadly, only 185 bodies were recovered. On 12 December 1866, several explosions caused by the ignition of flammable gases resulted in 360 miners and rescuers being killed at the Oaks Colliery at Stairfoot, Barnsley. With accidents like these, and the influence of Chartism and the spread of other working-class movements, it was not surprising that Barnsley became a centre for Radicalism. Such a history made it inevitable that socially concerned writers such as George Orwell would draw inspiration from the town, as is evidenced in his *The Road to*

Wigan Pier. In 1887 Barnsley established its own football club, which is still known throughout the land by its nickname of 'the Tykes'.

Thankfully today, Barnsley is a peaceful, quiet town. Situated between Sheffield, Leeds and Doncaster, and bordering on the Peak District, it is popular with tourists who flock to such sites as Cannon Hall, Wentworth Castle Gardens and the ruins of Monk Bretton Priory. The weekly market, which was established in 1849, is reputed to be one of the best in South Yorkshire.

But Barnsley is also the place where many murders have been committed …

Chapter One

Bodysnatching in Barnsley

In the year of 1829 it seems that the whole world was in a state of alarm as the deeds of the Scottish resurrectionists Burke and Hare were being reported in the newspapers. Their crimes in Edinburgh were so notorious that they affected people throughout the rest of the country who had recently buried a relative. People were appalled by stories of newly buried bodies being dug up and sold to dissectors. Methods were put in place to prevent such a thing happening, such as keeping watch over a recently interred body until putrefaction had set in, rendering the corpse useless to medical schools. Others surrounded the graves with wrought iron railings, some of which can still be seen in our churchyards today. The crime of bodysnatching was thought to be so heinous that those people even suspected of being resurrectionists were hated and were likely to be subjected to mob violence. So when it was reported that a case of bodysnatching had been uncovered in Barnsley that same year, there was a complete state of panic around the town.

The crime only came to light due to the vigilant nature of a Barnsley police constable named John Gamble, who noted a strange man and woman walking about the town. His suspicions were aroused because the couple appeared to be without any employment or purpose. A few days later, on Tuesday, 3 February 1829, PC Gamble was still keeping a watchful eye when he saw the man leaving a box at the Courier coach office. When he enquired about it with one of the officials, the box was brought to him and he saw that it was addressed to 'Mary Jones, No. 1 Princes Street, Edinburgh'. The writing was almost illegible and Gamble asked the coach office official to contact the man to ask him to write out the label more legibly. A watch was kept on the office and later that day the constable saw the same man remove the box. He then followed him back to a lodging house belonging to Samuel Howarth. PC Gamble went into the house and enquired about the name of the lodger concerned, to be told that his name was William Yeardley. When Yeardley was summoned, Gamble demanded that he open the box. At first the man refused. Yeardley saw that Gamble was determined, and suspecting the hostile reaction of the townspeople if the contents had been revealed, he implored of the constable, 'Do not open it here.' When Gamble questioned him on the contents, he replied, 'It contains what you suspect to find.' Gamble arrested the man, along with an unnamed woman who lived at the lodgings and was posing as his wife, and who was suspected of being an accomplice. (Women were known to play an important part in bodysnatching; they were often seen following a funeral and making note of whereabouts in the churchyard the grave had been dug.) The property was searched and what were called 'the usual tools' carried by resurrectionists were found. It was reported that these consisted of a large shovel with a small handle, hooks, screwdrivers and other tools of 'this unhallowed crime'.

The couple were taken before local magistrates The Reverend Dr Corbett and Mr Joseph Beckett and it was then that the box was finally opened. At first it appeared to be full of hay, but at the bottom of the box was the naked body of what appeared to be a two-year-old male. It was reported that the child had been crammed into the box in such a way that his little body would not have moved during the bumpy coach journey to Edinburgh. A surgeon was called to examine the body, and he gave his opinion

A typical coach of the period.

that the child had died a natural death. No signs of violence upon the body were found, but there was also no evidence of the manner in which it had been removed from the grave. The police authorities ordered that a description of the child be circulated, and posters were put up at prominent places around the town. The child was said to have flaxen-coloured hair and had a well-nourished and cared for appearance. However, the one identifying feature was the presence of ringworm on the left side of the head. Ringworm, a fungal infection, was common in the nineteenth century; it leaves circular marks on the skin about the size of an old-fashioned half-crown. Today such a condition is easily treated with creams, but the only effective cure in those days was to cut off the hair around the section of affected skin. The child's hair had been cut off on the left side of the head.

Yeardley and the woman were brought into court on the morning of Wednesday, 4 February, where he was described as 'a professional resurrectionist'. The landlord of the lodgings where the couple lived was called to the stand, and it was reported that he was 'an inoffensive working man'. Samuel Howarth told the jury that when the couple came to live with him he was not aware of their trade. They had lodged in his house for two to three weeks, and during that time he noted that they had taken delivery of two hampers and a large wooden box. During their detention the pair had refused to answer any questions as to where the body had come from, but Samuel Howarth told the magistrates that his lodgers had received a basket from Sheffield on the night of Monday, 2 February. Therefore he assumed that this was the town where the child had been taken from. The couple were remanded. When the news of the arrest of the resurrectionists was reported, it was said that many grieving relatives in Barnsley went to the churchyards to see if any of their dead had been removed. Incredibly it was found that two or three bodies were missing, and it was feared that the same bodysnatchers had been operating in Barnsley for some time.

Yeardley was brought before the two magistrates once again on Thursday, 5 February, although it seems that this time his female accomplice had not been detained. The magistrates considered that as she was his wife, she was deemed to be not guilty by being forced to act under his influence. By now the case was being discussed openly on every corner of the town, and as a consequence the room in which the court had gathered was 'crowded to excess'. So great was the curiosity that people in the courtroom peered closely to see William Yeardley emerge into the dock. He was described as being:

> a decent looking man about 5 feet 4 inches tall. His face was marked with smallpox and he had round features, light sandy hair and whiskers. His hands were white and delicate, which proved that for many years, he had little employment excepting for a short time at midnight. He has been seen occasionally in both Barnsley and Sheffield during the last three years.

Meanwhile, the body of the child had finally been identified. A surgeon, Mr Flather, of Attercliffe, Sheffield, attended the court and told the magistrates that the body was that of a child named Bagshawe. He had attended the family in his last illness and had been present when he died. Since hearing of the crime Mr Flather and the child's father had visited Attercliffe Cemetery and found the grave disturbed and the body missing.

The gates of Attercliffe Cemetery.

He had examined the empty coffin and the grave goods that had been buried with the child. They had been cast aside and the grave was left in some disorder. The bereaved father was a working man named Mr George Bagshawe. He too came into the magistrates' court and told them that his son had been seventeen months old and had died of an inflammation of the lungs. The child had died a fortnight previously, on Monday, 24 January, and had been buried at Attercliffe on the following Wednesday. George Bagshawe told the court how he had read the description of the child in a local newspaper and realized that it must be his son. The distraught father had formally identified the body at Barnsley on 3 February. George Bagshawe was very distressed as he told the court that the child's mother had been so grief-stricken at her son's death that she too had since died. At this point Dr Corbett asked Yeardley if he had anything to say to Mr Bagshawe, but Yeardley appeared to be quite unabashed as he replied, 'Nothing.' Dr Corbett ordered that the constable accompany George Bagshawe back to Attercliffe Cemetery and arrange for a second respectful interment of the child. He stated that the expenses would be paid for by the county.

Graves in Attercliffe Cemetery, where George Bagshaw's son was reburied. The reburial was paid for by the Barnsley Parish authorities.

Samuel Howarth said that he knew of a man named Bradshaw, a weaver in Barnsley, who had buried a 4-year-old child about ten days previously. On the very night of the child's funeral, Howarth stated, the prisoner and the woman had been out until well after midnight. The next morning he knew that Yeardley had sent a box to Edinburgh. Dr Corbett summed up the case for the jury, who returned a verdict of guilty. Yeardley was sent for trial at the assizes in Pontefract and Dr Corbett made reference to the death of Mrs Bagshawe, as he told the jury that the prisoner had 'been found guilty of violating a grave, but was also morally answerable for the crime of murder, since the violence with which he stood charged had led to another premature death'. He referred to the debate between the need for anatomical subjects and the greed of men such as Yeardley who were guilty of supplying that need. He stated:

> People can talk all they like about the interests of science and the necessity of diffusing anatomical knowledge, but better that dissecting rooms are empty rather than the feelings of mankind should be violated. Take away that hallowed feeling and veneration for the grave which men entertain, and much will be done to brutalize them.

Such was the anger against the crime that when Yeardley emerged from the courtroom he was surrounded by an angry, shouting mob, and it was only with the greatest difficulty that the police were able to protect him. It later appeared that other accomplices, a man called Peter Steward and his wife, had also been arrested. They had travelled on the coach from Barnsley to Edinburgh ten days previously, when Peter Steward had been seen carrying a hamper and a box. After the revelations of the past few days it was supposed that the box might have held two dead bodies. When Peter Steward and his wife returned to Barnsley on Friday, 6 February, he enquired at Samuel Howarth's lodging house for the Yeardleys and was swiftly taken into custody.

When the news that two more resurrectionists had been found in Barnsley, the local people were whipped into a fury that such criminals had been resident amongst them. Local newspapers stated that 'these people were suspected of being the same gang that had infested Sheffield and its neighbourhood for many months'. Others claimed: 'We regret to state that the churchyards of Barnsley have been plundered of their dead to a very great extent.' Correspondents wrote to the newspapers blaming the medical men who were paying for these bodies, and demanded that the dissection of a human body be made into a capital offence. Other correspondents recorded that William Yeardley had been seen in and around Sheffield on many occasions. Two letters about the case appeared the following week in the *Sheffield Independent* dated Saturday, 21 February 1829. One wrote:

> Since the Burke proceedings became the theme of local conversation, I have often heard persons dogmatize 'Oh he has murdered at least forty and the doctors all know about it. … I suggest that the surgeons knew about Burke, and were therefore well aware of where the bodies came from.

The letter was signed 'J.L.', and the tone repeated what the people of Barnsley were thinking. Another letter in the same newspaper questioned 'the need for medical schools' at all, stating that 'for as long as they exist such crimes will continue'. The writer felt that people 'would prefer to be wounded, maimed and living, in order to have the consolation of resting quietly in our graves when dead'.

The three prisoners were brought to the Pontefract Sessions on Friday, 1 May 1829, charged with 'disinterring the body of a male child at Attercliffe'. The chair of the sessions was William Battle Wrightson Esquire, of Cusworth. The three prisoners were Peter Steward, Mary Steward and William Yeardley. The defence was Sir Gregory Lewin and Mr Maude outlined the case for the prosecution. He described how the constable had found the body of the child at Barnsley, which had later been identified by its father. The gravedigger at Attercliffe, John Hobson, gave evidence that the grave of the child had been disturbed and the body had been taken out. Addressing the jury, the chair pointed out the necessity for a supply of anatomical subjects in order to further the interests of medical science, before returning to deal with the case in hand. Sir Gregory Lewin maintained that there was simply not enough evidence against Peter Steward, and that as Mrs Steward had been acting under the control of her husband, the case against them both should be dismissed. He concluded that for those same reasons the jury should acquit all the prisoners. Despite his eloquent defence, however, all three prisoners were found guilty but the sentencing was deferred until the following day. When the prisoners were brought before the court once again for judgment, the chair stated that there had been a judicial discussion in the case of Mary Steward. It had been agreed that she had been acting under the influence, and in the presence of, her husband, and that the case against her be dismissed. Unbelievably, it was agreed that as punishment she would pay a fine of one penny. The two other prisoners, Peter Steward and William Yeardley, were each sentenced to twelve months' imprisonment.

Such was the uproar about the case, rumours that resurrectionists were still operating in the area around Barnsley quickly circulated. As early as a month prior to the commencement of the trial on 25 April, it was reported that the body of a young woman had been stolen from her grave at Maltby. Friends of the girl had remained to watch over her body for three nights after her interment. Despite their vigilance, on the fourth day shavings were found at the side of the grave, which had been quickly spotted by the clerk to the parish. He caused the grave to be opened and they found that the girl's body was gone. The magistrates issued warrants and surgical institutions were searched in the towns of Sheffield and Rotherham, but nothing was found. The approbation against these bodysnatchers continued for many years, but thankfully they remained mainly conjecture. There is little doubt, however, that it would be a long time before grieving relatives ceased to worry about their recently deceased, and kept a sharper eye on the places where they were buried.

CHAPTER TWO

Murder of a Farmer

Every week, farmer George Blackburn would go into Barnsley to collect the money from his milk round. He was a man of regular habits and would leave his home at Elmhurst Farm, Banktop, and take the Sheffield Road into the town. Blackburn was aged fifty-seven and married, and the couple were very highly respected in the neighbourhood. On Monday, 5 October 1840, Blackburn was returning home at about 7.00 pm, as was his usual habit. Accompanied by a friend, the two men separated at the gate leading to the farm, which was almost opposite Mount Vernon Barracks. His servant, a girl called Emma Fretwell, was at the door of the brewhouse washing out a tub when she saw Blackburn coming down a path leading to the farm. She watched and saw him speak to two men in the stackyard, and Emma heard him say to them, 'What are you chaps doing there?' One of the men answered him, saying,

Sheffield Road, on which George Blackburn travelled into Barnsley.

'Damn thee, we will soon let thee know.' The horrified girl then saw one of the men jump up onto a wall and, picking up a large coping stone, he threw it directly at the old farmer's head. Blackburn was knocked to the ground from the blow, but with great determination he pulled himself up and staggered a few more paces before falling to the ground once more.

As he got to his feet a second time, Emma watched appalled as she saw another man appear from the stackyard and proceed to beat Blackburn with a large piece of wood. The man then smashed him in the face with the wood, dislocating his jawbone. Blackburn's wife, Ann, ran to the door when she heard the servant scream, and both women watched in horror as the farmer desperately tried to avoid the blows and attempted to reach his home. Running towards the injured man, Ann screamed out 'Murder!' and her cries brought out the sentry from the barracks at the top of the path. Seeing what was happening, the sentry raised the alarm. Several soldiers came out of the barracks whilst Ann pursued the men, screaming at the top of her voice, 'Oh, you have murdered my husband.' On seeing the approach of the soldiers and the angry wife, the three men ran away across the fields. The captain of the barracks, Captain Teesdale, dispatched some of his men to carry the poor man into his house, as he was by now bleeding badly and quite insensible. The captain mustered more of his men and ordered that a search be made for the escaped villains, and several of them spread out in all directions, searching the surrounding fields, woods and plantations. Another officer, Sergeant Speed, mounted his horse and went for a doctor, but Blackburn died soon after the doctor's arrival, at about 2.00 am on Tuesday morning.

The police were called and they joined the solders in searching the surrounding area. The large coping stone was picked up and when it was weighed was found to be almost 10½lbs. The large piece of wood, which was thought to have come from a five-bar gate, was also identified as that which had been used in the attack. It was 5 feet long, about 4 or 5 inches thick, and was a fearsome weapon. The police authorities deduced that robbery was the motive, but the cries of the farmer's wife and the servant girl had given the robbers no time or opportunity to carry out their intended act. Emma Fretwell told the police that before her master approached, she had seen two men whom she did not recognize hiding in the hedge. She described how they had emerged when the farmer was less than 50 feet from his home, before attacking him and knocking him to the ground. She told the police that a third man had rifled his pockets. An inquest was held on Wednesday, 7 October at the Horse and Jockey public house at Ward Green, Worsbrough, by coroner Mr Thomas Badger Esquire. The first witness gave evidence that George had been in Barnsley that afternoon collecting his milk money. Emma Fretwell described the attack once again. She told the coroner that after her master had been brought into the house, she had gone out with a candle and found his milk book and some coppers lying in the lane. Ann Blackburn described how her husband died and said that she took his head in her arms, but he was unconscious and unable to speak. Two doctors, Messrs Wainwright and Crooks, gave evidence that they had completed a post-mortem on George Blackburn, and the cause of death was from fractures to his skull as a result of the injuries received. At that point the coroner adjourned the inquest to Thursday, 15 October.

It was noted that curiosity about the case had resulted in the area around the public house attracting many people, to such an extent that the inquest officials could only leave the court with great difficulty. Police enquiries established the names of the men suspected of being involved in the robbery. Later that day a man named John Mitchell, aged seventeen, was apprehended and arrested in Shambles Street, Barnsley. When he had been brought into custody, Mitchell's trousers were examined and blood was found on them. Another man – George Robinson, aged twenty-three – was arrested in a common brothel on the same evening. The two men were taken into custody by PCs John and Thomas Carnelly (father and son) on suspicion of being involved in the crime. They were brought before the magistrate the same day and were remanded. On Friday morning at 2.00 am another suspect, William Fox, aged twenty-three, was taken into custody from his father's house at the Old Town, Barnsley, from where it seems that he had been missing since the murder. Police constables had kept a close watch on

Shambles Street, where John Mitchell was arrested for the murder of George Blackburn.

the property and he had been arrested when he returned to it. On the same day as the inquest was adjourned, the funeral of George Blackburn took place at St Mary's Church, Barnsley, attended by a very large congregation.

On Thursday, 15 October 1840, the inquest was reopened, this time at the Red Lion Inn at Worsbrough. The inn had a larger capacity and so more people could be fitted into the room. Among the people in the inquest room were several prominent men of the town. On the magistrates' bench was W. Newman Esquire, of Darley Hall, W.B. Martin Esquire, The Reverend H.B. Cooke, of Darfield, and The Reverend John Andrews, the incumbent of Worsbrough. Once again, several witnesses gave evidence that the three accused men, and another called Thomas Cherry, had been seen meeting in several public houses around the town. Other witnesses gave evidence of their proximity to where the robbery had taken place. A man called Joseph Mosley stated that he had seen Mitchell in company with a woman called Deborah Topping, seated on some steps on the Sheffield Road at about 6.15 pm on the night of the murder. Mosley told the coroner that from where Mitchell was sitting, he would be able to see anyone coming along the road from Barnsley to Worsbrough. A witness called William Middleton stated that he

St Mary's Church, where the body of George Blackburn was buried.

had seen two men running away from the direction of George Blackburn's house on 5 October. He watched as the two men escaped over a wall on the opposite side of the road.

A publican's wife, Jane Rollinson, of the Butcher's Arms, stated that Fox, Mitchell and Cherry had gone into their house on the night of the murder and asked for some bread and cheese. They stayed in the pub until 10.25 pm, although Fox had left before the other two went out. PC Francis Batty produced the trousers worn by Mitchell and showed the jury the marks that looked like blood on each leg of the trousers. He also described some shouting that had gone on between the men the day before, while they were being held in the prison cells, about the identification made by Emma Fretwell. Mitchell began singing and Robinson called out to him:

Robinson: 'Hello you. Who are you?'
Mitchell: 'It's me.'
Robinson: 'Have they got thee then?'
Mitchell: 'Aye, but there's nothing against me. When they took me before the magistrates, the girl did not know me.'
Robinson: 'They have had me up at Hilltop and the girl swears to me, and she'll swear to thee tomorrow.'

PC Thomas Carnelly told the court that he went to arrest Fox after hearing that he had returned to his parents' house. When he knocked on the door, it was answered by Fox's mother, who told him that she did not know where her son was. Entering the house, he spotted Fox's jacket, and when he went upstairs he found a pair of trousers and some stockings by a bed. He described how he came back downstairs and saw Fox's mother standing in the kitchen in front of a stone table, and when he pulled her to one side he found Fox, wearing only his shirt. When charged, Fox said he knew nothing about the murder and that he could 'clear himself', but he made no resistance as he was taken into Barnsley. The three men were then brought into the room, where they lined up with several other men, and Emma Fretwell was invited to pick out the men who had murdered George Blackburn. After looking steadily for some time, she pointed to the prisoner Mitchell, and then she hesitated before pointing out Robinson, saying that she believed him to be the other man. Mrs Ann Blackburn then came into the room and was asked the same question. She too pointed to Mitchell, but said that she could not positively identify the other two men.

The coroner then read out the evidence of the other witnesses. Cherry's brother, and two other men called John Jessop and George Barlow, swore that Robinson had been in their company on the night of the murder. The men claimed that they had been in a beerhouse called Wine Shades in Barnsley from 6.50 pm to 7.15 pm. Fox called several witnesses who stated that he had been at Bald Hey's beer shop in Barnsley on the same night. The coroner then adjourned the inquest to the following day, as it had already lasted eight hours. He stated that the government had offered a reward of £100 with a free pardon to any accomplice who may come forward and give evidence that would lead to the arrest of the principals in the crime. He also told the inquest that a subscription had been started in order to augment that figure by the principal gentry in the town.

The inquest was resumed the following morning and once again the room was filled with reverend gentlemen and landowners of the area. Added to the eminent men from the previous day were The Reverend H. Watkins, Vicar of Silkstone, W.B. Martin Esquire, of Worsbrough Hall, and William Clarke Esquire, of Harborough House. It was reported that the road all the way to Worsbrough Bridge was lined with spectators. The evidence was much the same as the day before, apart from that of the beerkeeper's wife, Dorothy Hey, which totally contradicted what she had said before. She swore that Fox had been in the beerhouse earlier than she had stated and that he was there at about 6.30 pm talking to two men at the door and had gone before 7.00 pm. She admitted that Fox's parents had asked her to say that he was in the house at the time of the murder, playing at cards. As she gave this evidence she appeared to be rather intimidated, and the coroner reassured her 'not to be deterred from telling the truth, for we will give you protection'. She told him that since she refused to swear to Fox being in the house, she had met Fox's parents in the street, stating that 'they abused me very much'. Her husband, Bald Hey, then took the stand and corroborated his wife's evidence.

In total, there were sixty-six witnesses, most of whom stated that the four men had been seen in and around Blackburn's house on the night of the murder. The farmer's wife, Ann Blackburn, was present in the room and appeared to be very much dejected as she listened to the evidence. The coroner summed up for the jury and they retired at 6.00 pm, and returned back at 7.05 pm. They found unanimously that Mitchell and Fox were guilty of the murder of George Blackburn and Cherry and Robinson were guilty as accessories before the fact. As the foreman of the jury returned the verdict, Robinson turned very pale, although the other three appeared unmoved. On Wednesday, 21 October 1840, it was reported that PCs Green and Carnelly took all four prisoners to York Castle to await their trial at the assizes.

The trial of John Mitchell, William Fox, George Robinson and Thomas Cherry began on Friday, 19 March 1841 at York, in front of the judge, Baron Rolfe. Because the case had been so well publicized, the judge warned the jury that they had to dismiss from their minds all they had heard previously, and to judge the case solely on the evidence that was to be heard in the courtroom. A total of twenty-five witnesses gave evidence regarding seeing the men near to the farm, and Emma Fretwell and Ann Blackburn once again identified Mitchell as the man who had thrown the stone. The defence, Mr Cottingham, threw doubt on the evidence, quoting cases of mistaken identification. He stated that there was simply no evidence that Mitchell was within three-quarters of a mile of the farm. He reminded the jury that they must be clear on the facts, telling them:

> The effect of your verdict must be irrevocable; and if afterwards it should be proved that you have erred, what would be your feelings? You must give an account hereafter of your conduct in this world; and if you err now, the spirit of this youth might appear to confront you and ask how you had dared on imperfect evidence, to cut him off in the prime of his youth.

Fox's defence, Sir Gregory Lewin, also warned the jury of the 'awfulness of their deliberations involving the life or death of a fellow creature', before pointing out the weakness in the case against his client.

Finally, the judge summed up and the jury deliberated for only a quarter of an hour before bringing in a guilty verdict against Mitchell. Fox, Robinson and Cherry were found not guilty and acquitted, and they were ordered to stand down. Then the clerk faced Mitchell and asked him if there was any reason why the sentence of death should not be given to him. Suddenly, as he spoke, nature seemed intent on having her say. There was a tremendous crash of thunder and a storm of hail and rain from outside, and a great darkness descended on the court. The noise of the rain was so bad that the proceedings were temporarily suspended until there was a lull. But while the people in court looked in wonder at each other at these events, Mitchell alone remained unmoved. In strong tones, above the noise of the storm, the judge gave Mitchell the sentence of death.

It seems that after a couple of visits from the prison chaplain while in the condemned cell at York Castle Prison, Mitchell changed in his demeanour. He later confessed that he was one of the men in the stackyard, but stated that it was one of his accomplices that had thrown the stone. Mitchell told the prison chaplain that he had thought he would get off with a custodial sentence, and had been shocked when he was sentenced to death. An application was made for clemency due to his very young age, but nevertheless the date of the hanging was set for Saturday, 10 April 1841. Just a week later, the governor of York Prison received a letter from the Secretary of State reprieving John Mitchell and sentencing him to be transported for life.

Finally, Mitchell made a confession stating that William Fox had not been involved in the murder. He said that on 5 October he had met with Cherry, Robinson and Fox at the village called

The condemned cell at York Castle Prison, where Mitchell was imprisoned.

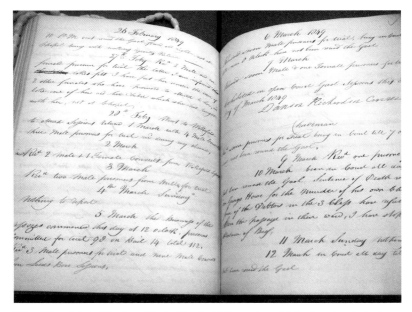

The Chaplain's Book at York Castle Prison, in which the chaplain kept notes of conversations with condemned prisoners.

Smithies around 10.00 am. The meeting had not been arranged and he claimed that the four had met by accident. He had met a girl called Deborah Topping and they made arrangements to see each other later that evening, around 5.30 pm. When they met, Mitchell claimed that he and the girl had spent some time together before bumping into Robinson and Cherry again. At this point Robinson told him that he wanted to talk to him, and the girl left. Robinson told him that George Blackburn, who had been collecting milk money, would pass Crow Well Hill and the three men set off in that direction. There was no sign of the farmer at the hill and so they went further. When they got to Banktop, Cherry grabbed a piece of wood, which was a gate top, and gave it to Mitchell, telling him to strike the man with it. He was with Cherry when he saw Robinson standing on the wall with a large coping stone in his hands.

Mitchell described the scuffle that followed when the farmer appeared and said that he had hit out at the man, but had hit Robinson instead. He saw Cherry run away and he claimed that was when he first saw the body of George Blackburn lying on the ground. Then he claimed that the three men went to the Butcher's Arms and had some cheese and bread, and some ale. Later he had spoken to Robinson, who told him that when he returned home he found his parents were in bed. Robinson said that his mother had got up to let him in, and his father told him that there had been a murder at Banktop. He asked his son where he had been and Robinson told him that he had been at Smithies all night. After he went to bed he heard his father praying out loud, saying that he hoped that the man who had committed the murder might be taken the next day. Mitchell stated that Robinson was arrested at about 2.00 pm on the very day that his father had predicted. John Mitchell had lived a life of criminality and he told the chaplain that he had committed 'a thousand robberies' and seemed unrepentant after his confession. He was one of 350 convicts who boarded the ship *Barrosa* on 27 August 1841, and set sail to Van Diemen's Land, now Tasmania, to start his life in exile.

CHAPTER THREE

Death of a Boatman

In the nineteenth century canals were the lifelines of industry. Roads were particularly poor and many independent bargemen would transport goods from one place to another. Such an independent boatman was Joseph Squires. On Friday, 26 March 1857, he left his house in Walmgate, York, and travelled from the city carrying a load of coal. Approaching the Barnsley Canal, Squires tied up at the Cawthorne Basin, where he hired two boys to watch the boat for him while he headed into the town to enjoy a few drinks. Joseph, who was aged about forty, had money to spend and a few hours later he had visited several public houses. In one of them he had met up with two other men known as William Barrett and 'Rag Jack'. At about midnight they went to the Wire Trellis public house on May Day Green, Barnsley, and called out for beer and a supper of oysters. The landlady, Mrs Mirfin, noted that the men appeared to be

May Day Green, where the Wire Trellis public house was situated.

on good terms with each other, but they only stayed in the inn for about an hour. Rag Jack was the first to leave, being ejected by the landlord for his drunken behaviour, whilst Squires and Barrett remained in the bar, where they could be seen by some men seated in the kitchen.

John Mirfin, the pub landlord, noted that Barrett kept going into the kitchen, where he had a short conversation with a notorious man called William Ellicker, who sat with four or five other men. They held a quick, muted conversation, after which Barrett rejoined Squires in the taproom area. A neighbour of Barrett's was a woman called Mary West, who was woken that night by someone throwing pebbles at the window of her lodgings. When she looked out she saw Barrett indicating that she should come downstairs. West went down and opened the door to her lodgings, and he told her to 'come here'. When she approached him he told her that there was a waterman at the Wire Trellis who 'had a good bit of brass on him'. He promised that he could get her two or three shillings if she went with him back to the pub. But West decided against it and went back to bed. John Mirfin noted that when Squires finally left the pub, Ellicker and some of the other men followed him. Later, in the early hours, Barrett returned back to the Wire Trellis and was supplied with some rum and two shillings worth of beer, which he said he was taking to Ellicker's house.

A woman called Hannah Wilson, who lived next door to Ellicker, was wakened around 3.00 am in the morning of 27 March by the sound of a woman screaming. She assumed that it was Elizabeth Fawcett, who lived with Ellicker, as the couple had frequent rows. Then she heard the sounds of a fight or scuffle before hearing the woman calling out, 'Oh Bill, pray let him alone,' and she heard Ellicker reply indignantly, 'He has given me a black eye.' Ominously she heard Fawcett say to him, 'Thou's done worse at him; pray at least get him a sip of water.' Hannah Wilson's son had been recently injured in a pit accident, and she left the house shortly afterwards to go to take care of him. Passing her neighbour's house, she heard no more noise or shouting and she proceeded on her way, and forgot all about the altercation. When she returned at 5.30 am, however, she saw the body of a man lying under her neighbour's window.

She did not recognize him and he seemed to be asleep, although she noted that he had blood at the back of his head. In an area where fighting and domestic abuse was a regular happening, once again she thought no more about it.

Another neighbour of Ellicker's was a woman called Mary Rusby. She too heard a lot of noise coming from next door at about 3.00 am, which she later described as being a lot of drunken men quarrelling. Annoyed by the brawling, Rusby got out of bed and opened her bedroom window. She saw William Ellicker throw a man out of his house, and saw the man, who she did not know, fall backwards, landing on the floor with his head against the wall opposite. Rusby watched as Ellicker made no attempt to help the man, but simply stared at him for a moment before he went back into his house and closed the door. She too was concerned about the man and so she pulled on a shawl and approached him carefully as he was lying in the street. Like her other neighbour, Mrs Rusby was reluctant to interfere, offering him no help as he seemed to be 'laying still enough'. A man called Andrew Holland was passing the house when he heard Ellicker order someone to 'get out' of his house. A man he couldn't see replied that he would not leave unless they returned to him something that he had lost, and once again Ellicker roared at him to 'get out'. As Holland approached he saw Ellicker and another man struggling at the doorway of his house. Ellicker appeared to swing the unknown man around, before he fell full-length in the street. Holland too did not interfere in what he presumed was yet another drunken scuffle. He went home to bed, but was awakened about 5.00 am when one of the pit lads knocked on his door to deliver a message saying that he was needed at the pit where he worked. As he was pulling on his work boots, the lad told him that there was a dead man outside. As he left his house in company with the boy, Holland saw the boatman lying on the ground, but he too did not approach him.

A chimney sweep called Joseph Wilkinson, of Plough Yard, Barnsley, was visiting a neighbour of William Ellicker when he heard a man demanding that he 'be given his cap and his handkerchief back'. He saw that there was another man he knew as John Newton also in the street, as well as a young woman. When he left the neighbour's house and set off for work at 3.30 am he saw the man just a few yards away. The man was still shouting at Ellicker, saying that if they gave him his cap and handkerchief he would go away. Ellicker came out and threatened the man that he would give him a black eye if he didn't go away at once. It was inevitable at this point that the attention of the police would be called to the disturbance. Police Constable William Hirst approached the noise and found the boatman, whom he later described as being 'dirty and disheveled', in the street. The man told him that he had been thrown out by Ellicker and that they had stolen some articles of clothing from him. PC Hirst took the man back into Ellicker's house, where he found several people, including Ellicker, his paramour Elizabeth Fawcett and her daughter, as well as others. He asked the people assembled there to attend to the man's head, which was by now bleeding profusely. He returned back to the police station and Inspector Green told him to call the police surgeon to the man at the house. When he went back Squires had once more been evicted from the property.

A few moments later, Police Constable John O'Neal, who had also been attracted by the shouting, arrived. PC O'Neal approached Squires, who complained to him that Ellicker had taken his coat, necktie, a ring and 11s 6d in cash. PC O'Neal found the man's cap lying on the floor outside the house, and he returned it to Squires, who at that time appeared to be unharmed. PC O'Neal and the boatman then went into the house with the chimney sweep Wilkinson closely following them. Ellicker asked PC O'Neal to remove the boatman, pointing at Joseph Squires. In front of the other witnesses PC O'Neal asked Squires again about the money that he had said had been stolen from him. In reply the boatman, who seemed confused, told him that he didn't have any money when he went to the house. Losing his patience by now, the policeman told Squires to 'go home and sober up'. He left to return back to his beat, and promptly forgot about the man, assuming, as the others did, that he was just another drunk.

In the early hours of Saturday, 28 March, at about 4.00 am, a man called William Wood, who lived in The Nook, Barnsley, heard someone enter his house. When he went downstairs he

A modern house on The
Nook today.

found Squires sitting in a chair. He was bleeding profusely;
blood was dripping onto his shoulders from his head. Wood
asked Squires what he was doing and the boatman asked him,
'Have I come into the wrong house?' Wood told him that he had
and Squires left. Finally, a little before 7.00 am, the boatman
was found in a bleeding condition by a good Samaritan. Squires'
saviour was a lodging house keeper named Thomas Leatham,
who also kept a house in The Nook. He saw the condition of the
man and he took him into his house, put him to bed and called
a surgeon. Dr Thomas Wainwright attended and found the man
to have a large wound on the side of the head and was quite
insensible. When he arrived the man was vomiting, and so the
doctor, who thought he had somehow ingested some poison,
gave him an emetic. The boatman vomited a large quantity of
matter, which the doctor noted was free from smell, before he
sank back against the pillows. Dr Wainwright decided that due to
the lack of smell from the vomit he had not been poisoned, and

deduced that he might be possibly suffering from concussion of the brain. He continued to visit Squires for several days before he died on Friday, 3 April 1857.

A few hours later, the man who had witnessed what he had thought was a drunken brawl – chimney sweep Joseph Wilkinson – was in the Railway Tavern having his breakfast. He saw Alfred Hargreaves, John Newton and three other men whom he had seen at Ellicker's house earlier that morning come into the tavern. Hargreaves approached Wilkinson and offered to sell him a silver ring, which he boasted he had obtained 'from a man's finger whilst shaking his hand'. Wilkinson refused to buy the ring, but later heard that it had been bought by one of the waiters at the Railway Tavern, a man called Charles Mason. He had bought the ring in exchange for giving Hargreaves a pint of ale and some tobacco. Later that week, on Wednesday evening, Hargreaves went to the pub and asked Mason if he could buy the ring back off him for a shilling. He stated that 'there would be some bother about it, as they got it from that boatman'. Mason was unable to oblige as he had given it to the landlady, who on hearing of the attack had passed it onto the police. Meanwhile, the police arrested William Barrett, William Ellicker, John Newton and Alfred Hargreaves, and they were brought into the Barnsley courthouse on Thursday, 2 April 1857. The four men were charged with brutally assaulting and robbing Joseph Squires, who at that time was still in a very dangerous condition and not expected to live. They were remanded, but on the following evening the boatman had more convulsive fits before he died at about 9.30 pm. The charge against the four men was now one of murder.

On Saturday night, 4 April, an inquest was held at the Court House in Barnsley in front of coroner Mr J. Taylor Esquire. Neighbours of Ellicker's gave evidence about hearing the uproar on the previous Saturday night. When one of the neighbours, Frances Hydes, appeared, she complained that she had been unable to sleep for the noise coming from Ellicker's house that evening. Hydes claimed that the walls were only a brick thick, and as a consequence she had heard Ellicker shouting at someone and telling him to get out of his house or he would kill him with the poker. She heard the poker rattle, followed by sounds of a fall and kicks and blows. The neighbour then heard the man say, 'Do you want to murder me?' before the sounds ceased and there was silence. A surgeon's assistant, Frederick Barrow, saw the man that he later learned to be Squires quarrelling with two men and demanding the return of his belongings at about 3.45 am that night, and he noted that the man was very drunk. Dr Wainwright gave evidence that he had treated the patient for concussion and had visited him daily up to his death. On the Tuesday morning he had found him to be 'almost sensible and able to give short answers to questions'. The surgeon asked him if he had lost a ring and he nodded. When asked what it was like he said it was a silver one. On the Friday he sunk once more into a comatose state before he died. Following the death of Squires, Dr Wainwright had been asked by the coroner to undertake a post-mortem examination. He found that the deceased man had an effusion of blood on the right side of his head, and the skull held a fracture that measured more than 11 inches in length. Dr Wainwright concluded that the man's death was due to having been hit on the side of the head with an object such as a poker, or there was the possibility that he might have been knocked down some concrete steps. The coroner then adjourned the inquest until the following Wednesday.

At the adjourned inquest PC John O'Neal gave his evidence and described how the deceased man was very drunk and unable to give an accurate account of how he had been robbed. He told the coroner that he was not wearing a cap or coat and complained that he had lost them together with a handkerchief and eleven shillings. Alfred Hargreaves had been standing next to him and when the policeman asked Squires where his clothes were, Hargreaves pointed to Ellicker's house and said they were 'in that house'. When PC O'Neal asked Squires again what had happened, the man appeared to be confused. The police constable advised Joseph Squires to return back to his vessel and come back in the morning. He told him that when he was sober, he might wish to take out a warrant against the parties who had assaulted and robbed him. PC William Hirst then gave evidence that he had received a silver ring from the landlady of the Railway Tavern. She had told him that barman Charles Mason had bought it from Alfred Hargreaves the day before.

The constable also produced a knife that had been found in William Barrett's pocket when he had been searched at the police station. When PC Hirst went to arrest William Ellicker and charge him with robbing and assaulting Squires, Ellicker had replied that he had 'given him no more than he deserved'.

The next witness was the deceased man's wife, Harriet, who had travelled down from the city of York, where the couple had lived. Despite the clear way in which she gave her evidence, she was very distressed as she identified the knife and the ring as the property of her husband.

When asked by the coroner if they wanted to speak in their own defence, the accused men individually made some long, rambling statements, which seemed to prove the guilt of William Ellicker. The jury found him guilty of manslaughter, and the other prisoners, William Barrett, John Newton and Alfred Hargreaves, were then discharged. After all the evidence had been presented, the inquest finally concluded at midnight.

William Ellicker was brought before the judge, Baron Channell, on Friday, 10 July 1857 at the York Assizes. On the previous day, Baron Channell had discussed the case and told the grand jury that he had looked at the depositions and found

York Castle Assizes.

that the death was 'occasioned partly by the blows, and partly by drink imprudently taken'. It was decided that there was a true bill (having enough evidence to prove the case) and that the trial would go ahead. The next day, Mr Wheelhouse outlined the case for the prosecution, describing the drunken row between William Ellicker and Joseph Squires. He claimed that Squires had been invited to a drink at the house and at some point had given William Ellicker a black eye. In retaliation, Ellicker attacked Squires with a poker, inflicting such 'a ferocious attack' that he died on 3 April. During the time he was injured, Squires was unable to give an accurate account of what had transpired. Although Ellicker had pleaded not guilty he admitted that he was wrong to have used the poker on the deceased man. He claimed that he had been attacked by Squires first when he had blacked his eye. The jury found him guilty and William Ellicker was sentenced to three months' imprisonment with hard labour.

CHAPTER FOUR

Poisoned for a Joke

S ometimes it is unclear whether murder was the actual motivation for a crime; in many cases a desire to scare was the intention rather than death itself. Such cases usually resulted in a charge of manslaughter rather than murder. A case that illustrates this was heard in Barnsley in March 1858, when a young man was accused of poisoning another. The tragedy was that this ended in the death of the accused, rather than the intended victim. Grocers Messrs Armitage of Barnsley employed two young men as assistants. For some time, one of the men, Frederick Heptonstall, who was aged twenty-two, had practically managed the branch at Silkstone. He had been held in high favour by his manager, and had got on well with the other assistant, Benjamin Fawcett. That is, until the end of March, when for some unknown reason Heptonstall received his notice and Fawcett was appointed in his place.

Naturally there was much resentment at his replacement and Heptonstall felt his dismissal keenly. He was convinced that the reason for his discharge lay with Fawcett, whom he suspected

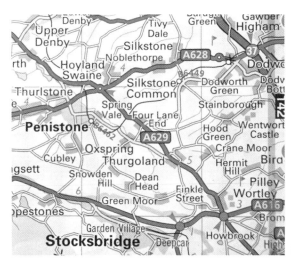

Map of Silkstone.

had been telling tales to his employer. In an attempt to get his own back, Heptonstall was determined to make Fawcett pay. On Saturday, 27 March 1858, with the two men still working in an air of seething resentment, the problem escalated and an argument broke out between them. Heptonstall went home that night with a grim determination to carry out his plan to full effect. He bought half an ounce of croton oil from Mr Joseph Mitchell, a druggist at Barnsley, on Sunday, 28 March. Croton oil is prepared from the seeds of a tree called *Croton tiglium*, which is cultivated in India. Taken internally, even small doses will cause diarrhoea, and no doubt this was Heptonstall's true intention.

The following day, when the two men were having a tea break at the shop, Benjamin Fawcett helped himself to sugar and put two spoonfuls in his tea, as was his habit. Soon afterwards he was taken very ill with a burning throat and the most violent stomach pains and diarrhoea. The smirk on Heptonstall's face told him everything, and he managed to get to a local doctor, Mr Ellis, of Silkstone, and told him that he had been poisoned. He also told him that it was Heptonstall who had poisoned him. He told the doctor that as he was the only one who took sugar, it was therefore probable that the poison had been put in the sugar bowl. He also knew that the only person that would have the opportunity of tampering with the sugar was Frederick Heptonstall. The doctor saw that his patient was in great pain and when he heard what he was saying he summoned another surgeon, Dr Jackson, of Barnsley, for a second opinion. As the poor man's pains increased in violence, the two doctors gave Fawcett an emetic, and then sent him directly home. Mr Ellis assured Fawcett that he would follow him immediately. When the surgeon arrived at Fawcett's home, however, he found his patient in complete agony. For many days both doctors felt sure that Benjamin Fawcett's life was in extreme danger.

The day after the poisoning, Frederick Heptonstall opened the shop as usual, and continued with his duties as manager. He gave no indication of concern even though he knew that Fawcett was seriously ill, no doubt convincing himself that his former colleague was putting it on in order to make him suffer. It was very probable that he convinced himself that Fawcett would indeed recover. At some point during the afternoon, Superintendent Burke called at the shop, and he showed Heptonstall the statement made by Fawcett claiming that he had poisoned him. When Heptonstall tried to explain that it had all been a joke, the superintendent showed him the doctors' evidence. They had analyzed the results of the emetic and found that Fawcett had been poisoned by a most unusual poison for that time. Police enquiries around the local chemists had proven that Heptonstall had in fact purchased the croton oil, and he was arrested. It was at this point that Frederick Heptonstall admitted that he had given Fawcett something that he had been told would make him very ill for a short while. He stressed that he had no intention of poisoning the young man. Superintendent Burke charged him and took him to the Barnsley Police Station, and there he took down his statement. Heptonstall admitted buying the croton oil from Mr Mitchell's shop. The young man seemed dazed by what was happening and told the superintendent that he did not know that croton oil was a poison, although he knew that it had been used in medicine. His lodgings were searched and a bottle of liquid found, which was established to be the remains of the croton oil.

The following morning, Wednesday, 31 March, Frederick Heptonstall was brought before magistrates Mr Thomas Taylor Esquire and The Reverend William Wordsworth charged with wilfully administering poison with intent to murder. Heptonstall stated that he had given Fawcett the croton oil with the intention of giving him 'a good scouring' due to the alleged stories that had circulated about him. Mr Ellis gave evidence that croton oil was a very dangerous substance to give someone, pointing out that even a small amount applied externally could cause irritation and swelling. The druggist Mr Joseph Mitchell confirmed that the prisoner had bought the oil from his shop. Mitchell produced the bottle and indicated how he had put the oil into it, filling it up to the shoulders. Mitchell demonstrated that about a third of it had been removed. Superintendent Burke told the magistrates that the remains of the sugar bowl had been sent for analysis to a surgeon from Leeds, Mr Scattergood. The prisoner was then remanded.

Heptonstall appeared in court in Barnsley again on Monday, 12 April 1858, before the same magistrates. On this occasion, Mr Newman appeared for the prosecution and Mr Hamer for the defence. Mr Scattergood appeared and told the magistrates that he had received 1,213 grains of sugar from Superintendent Burke. He also produced the bowl that had contained the sugar and had been kept on the shop premises. He told the court how he had examined these grains and found that they contained about seventeen grains of croton oil. Heptonstall's defence, Mr Hamer, stated that he was of the opinion that the case against his client was purely circumstantial. As far as he was concerned there was absolutely no evidence of any intention on the part of Frederick Heptonstall to poison Benjamin Fawcett. He maintained that his client had stated right from the start that the act had been carried out as a joke, and now exhibited great penitence for the injury he had inflicted on his colleague. Mr Hamer concluded by saying that because the young man claimed that this was just a prank, he hoped that the magistrates would not commit him to the assizes. The magistrates disagreed, and after a short consultation they ordered that Frederick Heptonstall was to take his trial at York on the capital charge of attempted murder.

There is little doubt that during the time that Heptonstall was confined to prison and was walking in the exercise yard while awaiting his trial, he had plenty of time to reflect on his foolish act of revenge. Certainly by the time the prisoner appeared at the York Assizes before Baron Martin on Friday, 16 July 1858, he seemed to fully understand the seriousness of his position. Mr Bliss QC and Mr Davison were the prosecution team and Mr Price appeared for Heptonstall's defence. Benjamin Fawcett, who was by now fully recovered, gave evidence of being taken ill after ingesting the sugar in his tea. Heptonstall barely looked up at his colleague as he made his statement. Mr Price claimed that the facts of the case did not prove that the intention of the prisoner was to do any kind of bodily harm to Fawcett, and he reiterated that to his client it had just been a foolish hoax. Mr Price claimed that when the prisoner bought the croton oil 'he believed that it was some kind of laxative medicine'. The defence's case was made more difficult by the

Exercise yard at York Castle Prison.

fact that there was no direct evidence of the defendant's guilt. To counterbalance this, the whole defence case was simply made up of witnesses who gave evidence of Heptonstall's previous good character. But the jury didn't see the joke and they found the prisoner guilty of administering the drug with the intent to seriously injure Benjamin Fawcett. They also gave a strong recommendation for mercy, due to the defendant's very young age. The defence counsel then brought up a legal objection as to whether this was strictly an offence or not. The judge consulted with his colleagues on the bench, but they were unable to agree. As a consequence, Baron Martin ordered that the prisoner was to be released for the time being on bail under recognizes of £20. He then ordered him to appear at the next assizes. Frederick Heptonstall left the dock reassured at this temporary reprieve, but undoubtedly wondering how things had gone so dramatically wrong.

On 13 November, the case of The Queen v Heptonstall was discussed in the Court of Criminal Appeal, before the Lord Chief Justice Wightman and Justices Williams, Hill and Baron Channell. The Lord Chief Justice stated: 'To kill a person by poison was as much an offence as running a man's body through with a sword.' Heptonstall's defence counsel, Mr Price, contended that no offence had been committed at common law or under the statute. He claimed that the prisoner simply intended to do his colleague no more harm than to cause him great discomfort. The Lord Chief Justice claimed that by 'using that argument, a most dangerous and atrocious act could be committed, and the guilty party would be allowed to escape without being punished'. After much discussion no decision was reached and the only conclusion they could come to was to reserve their verdict until the winter assizes, when Heptonstall would once again appear before them. There was uproar at this announcement, which to a lot of people seemed to be too important an issue to be 'fobbed off' in such a fashion.

In the end it was a mute point. On the morning of Sunday, 5 December 1858, Frederick Heptonstall, still out on bail, was found dead at Barnsley. Although there are no details as to how or when he had died, and despite his claims that 'it was all a joke', there was little doubt that his prank on Benjamin Fawcett had affected his mind. As the newspapers of the time stated, 'it had accelerated his death at only twenty-two years of age'.

CHAPTER FIVE

Poaching on Lord Wharncliffe's Estate

By the middle of the nineteenth century the crime of poaching was causing a national scandal. Many estate and landowners saw the crime as a serious threat to their property. Poachers, however, claimed that historically it had always been their right to eke out their living with game during the winter months. The crime took on new significance when estate owners appointed gamekeepers to watch over their lands. New game laws were introduced that brought in heavy prison sentences for men found out at night equipped to poach game. Many of the magistrates disagreed with the sentences and were more lenient when such crimes came before them. Discrepancies in the laws resulted in both gamekeepers and poachers arming themselves with bludgeons and shotguns. It was therefore inevitable that the crime of murder would be a result.

Lord Wharncliffe lived at Wortley Hall, near Barnsley, and employed several gamekeepers on his estate to protect his game. In December 1867, his head keeper was a man called George

Wortley Hall, where Lord Wharncliffe employed gamekeepers.

Thirkell, aged forty-five, who lived at Lower Pilley, situated on the Barnsley side of Wortley Hall. He had worked on the estate for five years and up to June of that year he and his wife had seven daughters and two sons. The two eldest daughters were both in service and no longer lived at home, but the other five sisters lived with their parents and their two brothers in a cottage on the estate. In an adjoining cottage lived another keeper, Thomas Oram, and his housekeeper. Thirkell came from a family of gamekeepers that had experienced many personal tragedies relating to their chosen career. His brother had been shot by poachers at Peterborough. Thirkell had been with him at the time, but managed to escape. A second brother, Harry, who had been an under-keeper at Wortley Hall, had accidentally shot himself at Grenoside about eighteen months previously. It was said that he was intoxicated at the time. He died instantly. Sadly, on the evening of Wednesday, 11 December 1867, George's run of misfortune was set to continue. Not only had he had lost his wife on 19 June that year, but his 18-year-old daughter had also recently died. For many years she had been subjected to fits, so her death was not unexpected. Nevertheless, George was devastated by the loss. Her body was due to be interred on the following day. No one realized at this point that the body of her father would soon be joining her.

It was at about 8.45 pm when another keeper, Tom Mayes, called at the cottage to tell George that four poachers had been seen in the neighbourhood of the estate. The keeper was intending to spend the night quietly at home with the funeral being the next day, so he was reluctant to go out. So he was reluctant to go out. Another man, James Hague, was also in the house, and he agreed to accompany Thirkell, Oram and Hayes to catch the poachers. Telling his sons that he would not be long, Thirkell left with the three men and they proceeded to the field where the poachers had last been sighted. They immediately spotted two men and as they closed in the keepers fired both barrels of a gun they carried with them. The two poachers had been engaged in recovering the nets they had previously set, and immediately raised up their hands in surrender. Thirkell leapt over the wall dividing two fields and attacked the nearest man with a bludgeon that he was carrying, and Oram felled the other. The poachers had a dog with them, which attacked the keepers. Thirkell instructed Oram to shoot the dog, but he only succeeded in wounding the dog, which quickly ran away. As this was happening, the poacher that had been bludgeoned by Thirkell got to his feet and ran off.

Thirkell then instructed Mayes and Hague to follow the escaping poacher and he returned back to where Oram was standing holding the second poacher. Thirkell started to gather up the nets in order to use them as evidence, when Oram asked the second poacher the name of the man who had run away. However, before the man had time to reply, three other men emerged from a ditch and Thirkell saw to his dismay that all three of them were armed. One of them went for Oram and he was knocked to the ground. A second poacher fired directly at Thirkell and the shot hit him square in the abdomen. The gamekeeper fell helpless to the ground as the two other men began to attack Oram with bludgeons. Thomas Oram tried to escape, but he was kicked brutally about the head and body. At the same time the other two keepers, Mayes and Hague, who had been chasing the fleeing poacher, heard the report of a gun and Oram's cries for assistance. They returned back to help the two gamekeepers, and seeing them arrive, the three poachers ran away. Oram and Hague went to the assistance of George Thirkell, who told them that he had been shot in the body, saying, 'I am a dead man.' Mayes and Hague stayed with the dying keeper while Oram ran for assistance. Tom Mayes was pretty sure at this stage that he had recognized the poachers, as he had had dealings with them before.

Oram ran to the nearest cottage, which was that of a collier named Stacey who also lived on Lord Wharncliffe's estate. He begged him to go to Thirkell's aid while he went to Park House Farm to rouse the owner, Mr John Sykes, who had retired to bed. In turn, the farmer roused his men, and one was dispatched to inform Mr Smith, His Lordship's steward, of the night's events, whilst another was ordered to bring a constable. A third was dispatched to bring a medical man. When Lord Wharncliffe heard what had happened he sent his own physician, Dr Alfred Marchmont Watson, to assist the dying man. Thomas Oram hurried back to aid Thirkell, but on the way was met with Stacey, who told him that the gamekeeper was already dead. Returning back to Park House Farm, Oram now got a horse and cart and, filling the cart with straw, went to bring the keeper's body back to the farm. It was reported that the whole of the process from when Thirkell had left his own house to being returned back to the farm as a corpse had taken only forty-five minutes.

The body of the dead gamekeeper was placed on a bed at the farm and covered with a sheet, ready for inspection by the police authorities, the coroner and the jury. Dr Wainwright arrived at the scene only to find that he was unable to do anything for the dead man. Lord Wharncliffe and his steward arrived next, and His Lordship ordered that messengers be sent on horseback to the police at Barnsley and Rotherham, informing them of the crime. A telegram was also dispatched to the Chief Constable of Sheffield, alerting him to the fact that there were several armed and dangerous men on the loose.

Police from all the different towns descended on the area and searched diligently for any evidence of the identity of the poachers. Several broken bludgeons were found at the scene, as was a strange hat, although it was noted that keeper Thomas Oram's own hat was missing. It was thought that one of the poachers had taken Oram's hat mistaking it for his own. Oram also told His Lordship that they had assumed there were only two poachers, and therefore they would not have fired both barrels, leaving the gun empty, before the three poachers emerged from the ditch. Local newspaper editors were informed that a reward of £50 was offered for information that would lead to the arrest of the men who had killed George Thirkell. The following day, Matthew Cutts was brought before Sheffield magistrates, charged with being one of the poachers involved. Cutts, who lived at Brightside, Sheffield, was described as being forty-one years of age, slightly small but stoutly built, with 'a round bullet head'. He was very inebriated when he was arrested at a public house, and when questioned remained mutinously silent as to his whereabouts over the previous few days. Only the previous Monday Cutts had been brought before the Rotherham magistrates charged with the same offence and he was remanded to Barnsley. The police also found a pawned gun that had belonged to George Thirkell. It was thought that the poachers had taken the gun in their flight immediately after the murder.

At 5.00 pm on Thursday, 12 December, Dr Thomas Wainwright, from Barnsley, and Dr E.M. Watson arrived at Park House Farm to undertake a post-mortem on the body of George Thirkell. On the following day, an inquest was also held at the farm by the coroner. George Oram described the night's events, and his testimony was followed by Tom Hayes, who corroborated his story. Dr Wainwright described how he had carried out the post-mortem on George Thirkell. He stated that externally he had found a protrusion of the bowels, but there were no other marks of violence visible apart from a few bruises on his arms and legs. Internally, most of the organs had been healthy, but for the left lung, which was slightly congested. Dr Wainwright said that he had found a lot of 'No. 8 shot' firmly embedded in the man's spine, and he had no doubt that the cause of death was hemorrhage. Dr Watson concurred with his colleague, and gave the opinion that with such injuries his death would have been instantaneous. The inquest was then adjourned until 30 December.

On Sunday, 15 December 1867 at noon, the bodies of George Thirkell and his daughter were buried at Wortley churchyard. There was a large attendance of local persons, who came from the towns of Sheffield, Barnsley and Rotherham. The funeral cortège of the murdered man was preceded by that of his daughter. The two coffins were followed by eight young persons all dressed in white with black scarves. George's surviving six daughters and two sons followed in a carriage, and a large number of other distinguished persons followed on behind. A few days later, an auction sale was held for the murdered man's children. Large crowds of buyers and sightseers attended the house at Pilley Bottom and watched as his household furniture was sold. Before the bidding started, the auctioneer referred to the sad event that had caused the sale to be held. He added that for that reason he hoped that the bids would be liberal. It was reported that among the collection of articles for sale were seven cases of stuffed birds, foxes and stags' heads, as well as two fine retriever dogs and five double-barrelled guns.

The inquest was reopened on 30 December at the Wortley Arms at Wortley, where a short conference was held by the legal representatives. It seems that no new evidence had come to light, apart from the arrest of several men suspected of being implicated in the murder. As the police authorities had not had time to question the suspected men the coroner informed the inquest that because no evidence had been adduced, the enquiry would be adjourned to 27 January 1868.

Meanwhile, Matthew Cutts was also brought up to the magistrates' court in Barnsley. Although he had already been in custody for seventeen days, no evidence was produced against him, and he was simply remanded yet again. Despite the terrible weather conditions, the courtroom and streets around the court had been packed with people, all anxious to hear the details of the crime. During this time the police were scouring the area and questioning known poachers in order to elicit the names of the other men that had taken part in the affray. Finally, on Monday, 6 January 1868, Cutts and two other prisoners were brought into the Barnsley courthouse. The two other men were named as Joseph English, aged thirty-three, and Joseph Beardshaw, aged twenty-six. All three men were charged with the murder of George Thirkell. They were described as being three 'very ordinary looking men' and that:

> Certainly their appearance is anything but what one would expect, when it is borne in mind that they are members of a most determined and desperate gang of poachers. English, the man who is said to have fired the fatal shot, and Beardshaw are the most determined looking, but they do not come up to the popular notion entertained of the build and appearance of night poachers. As for Cutts, he had a round, red, good-natured face and judging from outward appearances, one would fancy him to be the last man in the world who would go night poaching, and lend himself to deeds of violence.

The prosecution stated that in order to complete the case he would have to produce over forty witnesses, and the case would therefore take a full three days. Various witnesses gave evidence of seeing the men meeting together in different places, sometimes carrying 'bundles' and at other times without. The three men appeared to be unperturbed at their situation and were laughing and joking as the court broke up for lunch. The men all smiled and seemed at ease when Joseph Beardshaw's dog, named Smoke, limped into the courtroom on three legs. The next day, the enquiry heard evidence of the arrests and the men's confessions, and then the case was adjourned to Friday. When the court reconvened yet more witnesses were heard, and they gave evidence that placed the men close to where the murder took place. The most important witness, however, was Thomas Oram, who swore to seeing Joseph English fire the gun at George Thirkell. The prisoners were quickly found guilty and ordered to take their trial at the next assizes on two charges. The first was the more serious one of the wilful murder of George Thirkell and the second was for night poaching. The following day, the police arrested a man called Joseph Gregory, who was said to be the fourth poacher and was aged about fifty-one.

Leeds Town Hall, where the four poachers were tried.

On Friday, 27 March 1868, the four prisoners appeared at Leeds Assizes in front of the judge, Justice Hannen. A technical objection was made at the commencement of the trial that Lord Wharncliffe had not proved his right over the game, but the judge overruled it and the trial started. The amount of evidence was so huge that it took the prosecution all day just to present it. The judge adjourned the case to the following day in order to present his summing-up. The following day after the judge's conclusions, the jury found both Matthew Cutts and Joseph English guilty of manslaughter, rather than murder. They found Joseph Beardshaw and Joseph Gregory not guilty of the murder of George Thirkell, but simply guilty of night poaching. The judge appeared to be somewhat sympathetic towards the men as he sentenced English to ten years' and Cutts to five years' imprisonment. The two other men also received light sentences; Beardshaw was sentenced to eighteen months' and Gregory to fifteen months' imprisonment.

CHAPTER SIX

Death in a Hovel

Nineteenth-century housing in many towns and cities throughout the entire country was generally seen as poor, and Barnsley was no exception. Many people of the time had to sleep, wash, dress, cook, eat, work, live and die all in one room. Bearing in mind that most houses had little in the way of sanitary arrangements it is no surprise that overcrowding caused sickness. Naturally, living in such conditions caused tension, which led to brutal behaviour and, sadly, the most common crime of that period was that of domestic violence. In those days it was not a crime to beat your wife or your common-law partner. Many cases that did get to court simply resulted in a man being given a warning by the magistrate to moderate his treatment of his wife. Occasionally he would have to pay a surety for a period of time to be on his best behaviour, but there was little justice for a woman who cohabited with a man who beat her. That is, unless the case was so violent that it could not be ignored. Thankfully, in the second half of the century, when such a case resulted in murder it was treated as a capital offence.

Charlotte McReady was thirty-one in 1862, when she met and began cohabiting with a stonemason called John Harris. They had both been born and had lived in Scotland for most of their lives. Because of his Scottish heritage Harris was more familiarly known as 'Scotty Harris'. In 1866, McReady, now aged thirty-five, and Scotty, aged thirty, decided that they would move down south to the North of England, and they hoped to find work in Barnsley. The couple rented a house on Joseph Court, Wilson Place, where they lived with McReady's 9-year-old daughter, Ellen, the child of a previous marriage. The house in which they lived could only be described as a hovel as it was disgusting by any standards. A local newspaper reported that the living quarters were entered by a low passage leading into a court, and consisted of:

one room in which it was barely possible for a man to stand up. In one corner was a bedstead without a mattress, but just straw on which to lay, and in another corner was a rudely built stone table, which contained a broken water pot and a bowl. A small shelf acted as a cupboard on which were placed some earthenware pots and some meat from a previous meal. One chair and a stool and a small table were all that remained in the room. Most of the fixtures in the room had been broken and the door was off its hinges.

Living in such poor conditions it is not surprising that, like most people of the time, McReady and Harris found solace in alcohol. Their relationship was not harmonious due to them being hardened drinkers, and arguments were common. On Saturday, 4 April 1868, the couple had been drinking for most of the day at a pub called The Commercial on Summer Lane, Barnsley. They met up with two friends of Scotty Harris's, John Holdsworth and a man called Fox, who were invited to have

The Commercial on Summer Lane, where John Harris and Charlotte McReady drank for the last time.

supper with them. The three men and McReady went back to the squalid little room, where she boiled four pieces of haddock. Later, after Holdsworth and Fox had left, another argument broke out in which Harris accused the woman of stealing money from him and he struck her. As was usual in such circumstances, McReady gathered up Ellen and they fled to a house belonging to their neighbour, Mary Gardiner. McReady told her about the row and Mrs Gardiner agreed that she could wait at her house until Harris fell asleep. At around 2.00 am, McReady asked Mrs Gardiner to walk with her back to her own house to make sure that Harris had gone to bed. As they approached the hovel the two women could see through the broken door that he was asleep on the bed. McReady opened the door and went in and saw that in his drunken stupor Harris still had his boots on. Considerately, she got down on her knees to take off his boots, but it disturbed him and he lashed out at her with his feet. Mrs Gardiner ran into the room and tried to hold onto Harris to stop him hurting the woman, but he shook her off and proceeded to kick at McReady, who was now on the ground. The neighbour watched in horror as in a determined effort he stamped on her head with his heavy work boot. Mrs Gardiner was crying and pleading with Harris to desist, but he picked up a knife and so alarmed her that she ran out of the house. Mrs Gardiner returned home and pleaded with her husband to 'do something', but he warned her to leave the matter well alone, and she finally went to bed.

At about 6.30 am the following morning, there was a knock on the broken door from a man called John Wagstaffe. As he knocked, the door partially opened, and he pushed at it and went inside. There he found the body of the woman, and alongside her lay Scotty Harris. Wagstaffe woke up his friend, who took one look at the body of his former paramour and fled the house. The police were called and a search was made for Harris, who was found to have gone to Doncaster. Inspector Greenwood of the Barnsley Police and the witness John Wagstaffe were dispatched to Doncaster, where they searched the local pubs and lodging houses. Scotty Harris was quickly found and arrested for the murder of Charlotte McReady, to which he replied that he 'had never touched her'. With our modern awareness of the importance of the integrity of a crime scene, it was pretty horrific to read newspaper reports of the large number of curious people being admitted to the hovel. The body of the poor woman was still on display and it was reported that there was great excitement in the area. Finally the body was moved to the nearby Commercial inn, the last place that the couple had visited before the murder. The following day, Harris was brought into the courtroom at Barnsley before the magistrate Mr T.E. Taylor Esquire, and he was remanded.

The story of the brutal crime was quickly repeated through the town and, as a result, when the inquest took place on Tuesday, 7 April 1868, the streets all around the inn were crowded with thousands of people. All the roads leading to the public house were similarly crowded, and the coroner, Mr J. Taylor, was forced to push his way inside. Not surprisingly, the first person to give evidence was the neighbour, Mary Gardiner. She had identified the dead woman, whom, she told the court, had cohabited with the man known as Scotty Harris. Mary Gardiner spoke about the last time she had seen McReady, which was on the Saturday evening, at about 11.30 pm, and admitted that 'she was drunk, but not intoxicated'. The couple had been in the Commercial inn and had two pennyworth of rum each, and McReady had taken half a gallon of beer home with her. As a consequence, when she arrived at her neighbour's house at 2.00 am she seemed to be more intoxicated. Mary Gardiner told the coroner that the deceased woman stayed for about twenty minutes, before pleading with her neighbour to return back to the house with her.

Mrs Gardiner then described for the inquest the horrific attack that Harris had made on his former paramour. The boots belonging to the accused man were shown to the jury, and it was noted that they were heavy work boots. As the neighbour continued with her evidence she described how the man had kicked the deceased woman in the side, accusing her of stealing his money. McReady had made no reply, but after attacking her and while she was on the floor, Harris had reached into her bosom and taken out a little black purse with some money in, which he said was his. Mary Gardiner then stated how she had fled after he drew out the knife and threatened her. She had run out into Wilson Place and looked in vain for a policeman, but she was unable to find one. The following morning, when she was roused by John Wagstaffe, she went to the house and found her neighbour on the floor, lying in the same position as she had left her the night before. Another witness was John Holdsworth, who told the coroner about being with the couple on the Saturday night, when they visited several public houses in Barnsley. He agreed with the previous witness that McReady was tipsy, but not drunk. Holdsworth told the coroner that he had witnessed Harris giving her some money to buy some fish, and how he had gone home with the couple to share their supper. He stated that the little girl, Ellen, was in the room at the time and when he left at 1.30 am, McReady had not been injured in any way.

Next to give evidence was the daughter, Ellen, who was described as an 'intelligent-looking' child. She told the jury that on that Saturday night she had gone to bed and was awakened by the shouting, when she saw Harris kicking at her mother. She went to Mary Gardiner's house and she too went looking for a policeman, but could not find one. Scotty Harris had also threatened her, so she spent the night with an old woman called Sarah Yates who lived nearby. John Wagstaffe gave evidence of how he had arrived in the morning and found the body. When he woke Harris up and showed him the body the man bragged that he had 'finished her off at last'. When Wagstaffe told his friend that his actions might lead to serious trouble, it was only at that point that Harris seemed to realize the seriousness of his position. He asked him, 'What shall I do?' and Wagstaffe advised him not to run away. But he then went to the next-door neighbour's, and when he returned Harris had gone. The witness told the hushed inquest that he had noticed that Harris still had the woman's blood on his boots. At this point in his evidence the prisoner pointed to John Wagstaffe and shouted that he had found the body, and added, 'I never touched her, or did anything at her.'

Mr Thomas Wainwright, surgeon, told the inquest that the death of Charlotte McReady had been caused by a fractured skull. Gruesomely, he then produced a piece of the woman's skull, which he said had entered the brain and torn the vessels, which produced an effusion of blood. He stated that he had also examined the prisoner's boots and agreed that they would have caused the wound from which the woman had died. Inspector William Greenwood, of the Barnsley Police, described how he and Wagstaffe had found Scotty Harris and arrested him at Doncaster. The two men had then brought Harris back to Barnsley, where he was placed in a cell, and his boots were removed. When the prisoner was charged with murder he told the inspector that he had left McReady in the house drinking with two strange men. He stated that she was still alive when he left, and he knew nothing about her murder. The prisoner was unable to describe the two men, saying that he had never met them before.

The coroner, Mr Taylor, summed up for the jury, calling their attention to the evidence of Mary Gardiner, who had witnessed the attack, as had the little girl, Ellen. Both had attested that John Harris was drunk, but he told the jury that it did not give him a good reason for carrying out such a vicious attack. Mr Taylor stated that if the jury thought there were no extenuating circumstances, they would be bound to return a verdict of wilful murder. However, he told them that if they thought there were extenuating circumstances, the jury might find him guilty of manslaughter. The jury took just three quarters of an hour before finding the prisoner guilty of murder. On the following Thursday, the courthouse was crowded once again as James Harris was brought before magistrates The Reverend H.B. Cooke and T.E. Taylor Esquire. The evidence was the same as at the inquest, but the prisoner argued that all the witnesses had lied and 'had not told a grain of truth'. Despite the clear evidence of witnesses to the attack, his defence was that he was drunk, and knew nothing about it. The magistrates had no such doubts and the prisoner was committed to take his trial at the assizes.

James 'Scotty' Harris was brought to the Leeds Assizes in front of the judge, Mr Justice Lush, on Monday, 11 August 1868. Mr Wainwright, who had performed a post-mortem on the deceased woman, told the judge that McReady had died from the brutal violence to which she had been subjected. He told the judge:

She had severe wounds over both eyes, both injuries having gone down to the bone. The vessels at the back of the head were lacerated and may have been inflicted by a pair of heavy work boots, similar to those worn by the prisoner.

Harris's defence, Mr Bruce, stated that there had been no premeditation of the attack, and therefore the charge ought to be reduced to one of manslaughter. He claimed that when the deceased woman went to take off his client's boots, the prisoner was half asleep when he lashed out at her. He pointed out that Harris had told him that he had a knife on him, with which he could have killed her if he had wanted to. At this point the jury left the court and, after six hours of deliberation, Mr Justice Lush called them back into the courtroom. He asked the foreman whether there was any point of law which he could clarify for them that would make it easier for them to come to some decision. The foreman stated that the main sticking point was the belief that if they found Harris guilty of manslaughter, their understanding was that the judge would not be able to sentence him to more than two years in prison. They felt that the amount of violence used made it a much more serious crime.

Mr Justice Lush agreed; he told them that the crime of manslaughter was one to which there was so great a variance in punishment, which was left to the judge's discretion. He patiently explained, 'There is the widest range from one hours' imprisonment to penal servitude for life,' depending on the circumstances. The jury looked relieved and the foreman told the judge they would be able to agree in ten minutes, now that point had been cleared up. Without leaving the court they consulted in the box, before bringing in a verdict that James Harris was guilty of manslaughter. Mr Justice Lush told him:

If the jury had found you guilty of murder, I should have had no alternative but to pass on you the sentence of death, and it must then have been left to the advisers of the Crown to make any mitigation of your punishment. The jury, however, found you guilty of manslaughter, which is not now a capital offence. The punishment for that crime, as I have just remarked, varies more than that for any other, for manslaughter may vary in degree from the range of murder to the verge of justifiable homicide. I feel that your crime, although not murder, is the next approach to murder, and I therefore think I should not be doing my duty if I did not pass upon you the heaviest sentence.

He then sentenced Harris to life imprisonment. It was undoubtedly a vicious crime, which was exacerbated by the cramped and unsanitary way in which people were forced to live. Working-class houses were very low on the agenda of local councils and it was not until the 1920s and '30s that these slums were finally eradicated from the towns of South Yorkshire.

CHAPTER SEVEN

Was it Murder?

In the nineteenth century marriage was seen as an institution that was intended to last for a lifetime. Queen Victoria herself encouraged the notion of 'family values' and so women who lived separately from their husbands were looked down on from the so-called respectable society. Those who were known to receive 'gentlemen callers' were despised even more. Elizabeth Fairhurst was a 38-year-old Barnsley woman who slotted into the lowest category, simply because the lover who visited her regularly was married. Elizabeth lived at Naylor's Yard, Albert Street, whilst her paramour, Jesse Pickard, aged thirty-nine, lived with his wife at Smithies, which was a mile out of the town centre. The double standards of the day did not reflect any dishonour on him as he was a man who was well respected. Pickard worked as a foreman blacksmith at the East Gawber Colliery, where he had worked for the previous fifteen years.

A row of houses at Smithies.

He was in the habit of calling on the woman he called 'Lizzie' for two or three nights during the week. He usually returned on Saturday and would spend the weekend at her house, leaving her on Monday morning to go to work. What his wife thought of these arrangements is not recorded, but society's rejection, from which Elizabeth undoubtedly suffered, resulted, not unnaturally, in her being addicted to alcohol.

On the night of Sunday, 8 June 1873, a man named Rhodes had tried the door to Elizabeth's house, and finding it unlocked had entered the building. The door opened onto a set of stone steps that led up to her rooms. He noted that a chamber pot was at the bottom of the stone stairs and was broken into two pieces. Rhodes shouted out but received no reply, and going up the stairs he found Elizabeth lying dead on her bed. It was well known in the neighbourhood that Lizzie was fond of drink, and it was reported that she was often drunk for as long as a week or a fortnight. At the time Rhodes just presumed that she had died from intoxication. The surgeon, Mr Charles Henry Wainwright, was called to the house. He arrived at 10.30 pm and examined

Market Street, where William Bowrigg heard screams early in the morning of 8 June 1873.

the woman on the bed. The surgeon noted that Elizabeth had a severe fracture of the skull. The next morning, a friend and work colleague of Pickard's, named William Bowrigg, saw him arrive at the colliery for work at 5.30 am. He told him that he had been in Market Street early on Sunday morning and had heard a scream coming from the rear of the house where Lizzie lived. He asked Pickard if anyone had died or been killed in that building. Bowrigg had heard the rumours about Elizabeth Fairhurst and Pickard, and he was also aware that the man had a vicious temper. Pickard denied knowing anything about it and proceeded to get on with his work. But at around 10.00 am Police Constable Gamwell arrived at the colliery and asked to speak to Jesse Pickard. After a very short conversation Pickard was arrested for the murder of Elizabeth Fairhurst. In reply to the charge he told PC Gamwell, 'If it is so, it is and I can't help it now.'

That very same afternoon an inquest was called by the coroner, Mr J. Taylor, at the Trafalgar Hotel on New Street, Barnsley, and Jesse Pickard was in attendance. The first duty

New Street, where the Trafalgar Hotel was situated, where the inquest on Elizabeth Fairhurst was held.

for the coroner and the jury was to see the body of the dead woman in situ. Pickard, accompanied by two constables, was also taken to the bedroom where the dead body still lay. Although Pickard was closely watched, he made no sign as he looked at the body of his former lover. Mr Wainwright told the coroner that when he had examined the body the previous day, he found it cold and stiff and gave his opinion that she had been murdered between eighteen to twenty-four hours previously. He stated that the severity of the fractured skull would prove that the woman's death had been instantaneous. The coroner asked Mr Wainwright if a blow or a kick could have caused the death, and he agreed that either might have resulted in the same outcome, or it might have been caused by a fall. An elderly neighbour, John Fenton, who lived next door to the deceased woman, gave evidence that he last saw her at around 8.00 pm on the Saturday night. He told the coroner that she seemed to be pretty drunk, but he described her as being 'intoxicated, but happy'. The next morning, Fenton noted that her shutters were still closed, and being a neighbourly sort of person, at about 9.00 am he went next door into the downstairs rooms and opened them. He heard nothing more until he heard the noise of a lot of people at about 11.00 am. When Fenton went to enquire as to what was the matter, he found a number of people inside the house, and they told him that Elizabeth Fairhurst was dead. John Fenton went upstairs and saw the body, covered with a blanket, lying on the bed. The witness then identified the prisoner as the man he knew as Jesse Pickard, and stated that he had last seen him at the house two days previously.

Superintendent Sykes, of the Barnsley Police, was the next person to give evidence, and he told the coroner that he had heard the prisoner threaten the deceased woman on many occasions. This was usually after the couple had been arguing, and he had also seen her with bruises on her face and arms. At this stage the coroner, who had three other inquests that same evening, asked the surgeon to undertake a post-mortem on the body and the case was adjourned. The following day, the inquest was resumed and it was reported that the streets around the Trafalgar Hotel were crowded with sightseers. The surgeon, Mr Wainwright, stated that he had completed the post-mortem and found much blood on the inside of the skull. He also described the fracture wound, which measured about 5 inches in length and about 2 inches wide. Mr Wainwright explained that there was little or no swelling of the brain, which indicated to him that her death had been very quick.

Another resident of Naylor's Yard, Julia Beechill, stated that she too had seen Elizabeth on the Saturday night, standing at the door to her house. She also saw Pickard visit on the same night at about 9.00 pm, but remembered that he only stayed about ten minutes. The witness told the coroner that she saw him at the house again later in the evening and she had heard the couple arguing. She had taken little notice as both of them were heavy drinkers and she had heard them argue many times before. Perhaps on this occasion Elizabeth had finally had enough of her lover, Julie Beechill told the jury, because while passing the house she had heard Elizabeth say:

> Well Jesse, do what you think proper and go home to your wife and family. I won't have thee come any longer. I have kept open house long enough for thee. I don't want you here.

The argument seems to have developed because, despite his own huge alcohol consumption, Pickard was objecting to Elizabeth's drinking habits. Earlier that week her neighbour had overheard him tell her that if she drank any more beer, he would see to it that she would never drink another glass of beer while she kept his company. Julia Beechill told the coroner that the deceased woman had no other callers, but remarked that Pickard would often arrive after Elizabeth had gone to bed, and she was forced to get up to open the door to him.

Another witness, a neighbour of the deceased called Mary Beaumont, stated that she had heard Pickard arriving at the house at some point between midnight and 1.00 am. He found the door locked and bolted and he kicked savagely at it. The witness heard Lizzie open the bedroom window and shout down, 'Is that thee, Jesse?' He grunted some reply and then, almost immediately, she heard the door being opened by Elizabeth. Later still that night she heard a woman groaning, as well as a man's voice. Earlier she had heard Pickard say, 'Lizzie, if you do not give over drinking, I will kill you.' Another man who had known Pickard for over two years, a brickmaker named John Smith, stated that he had seen the prisoner coming from the direction of Barnsley to his own home at Smithies, at about 5.00 am on the Sunday morning. The men acknowledged each other, but had no conversation at that point. The coroner asked him how Pickard had looked at that early hour of the morning. Smith stated that he saw nothing wrong in the man's demeanor and thought no more about it. The coroner summed up for the jury, who took only two hours to find Jesse Pickard guilty of wilful murder. Crowds of people outside the hotel booed as the prisoner was removed and taken back into custody.

There was much discussion in the streets of Barnsley as to whether Jesse Pickard had killed Elizabeth Fairhurst at all. It was known that she was a heavy drinker and the sight of the chamber pot at the bottom of the steps led some to believe that she may have fallen down the stone stairs accidentally while drunk. The doubt in some people's minds was still evident on Wednesday, 14 August 1873, before the trial of Jesse Pickard was due to be heard at Leeds Town Hall. Judge Sir G.E. Honyman cautioned the grand jury before the case started and urged them to be completely satisfied that Elizabeth Fairhurst had died at the hands of Jesse Pickard. He told them:

> You must assure yourselves that the injury had not been caused by her falling down the stairs. It would appear that the body had been found on the bed, and therefore it was highly unlikely, but you must also take into account the chamber pot that was found inside the front door. Therefore before you can return a true bill of murder, you must be satisfied that death was the result of injuries inflicted on the victim with the intention of causing her death. However, if you feel that death was caused in a scuffle, you would be justified in returning a bill for manslaughter.

Although much of the evidence given by witnesses at the trial was the same as had been given at the inquest, there were some important changes. Neighbour Mrs Julie Beechill had previously stated that she had not seen the body of Elizabeth Fairhurst on the Sunday night, but the deposition that had been taken at the inquest categorically stated that she had. The statement written by the magistrates' clerk was read out to her. In it, Mrs Beechill had said, 'I saw her on Sunday night the 8th instant, lying across the bed, in her bedroom, dead.' She was challenged on this by the judge but she continued to deny having said it.

Even the surgeon, Mr Wainwright, now elaborated on his former statement. He once again gave his opinion that the wound could have been made by a blow or a kick, or it might have been caused by a fall down the stone steps. However, Mr Wainwright added that if such was the case, he did not think her capable of getting back up the stairs, if she had fallen down, due to the fact that the steps up to the bedroom were so steep. He did not add that the situation would have been exacerbated by her heavy drinking, but there was little doubt that it must have been in the jury's mind. When asked by the judge if he thought that it 'could have been a possibility, no matter how remote', he admitted that 'she might have done'. Other neighbours giving evidence stated that they had entered the house on the Sunday evening, where they had seen Elizabeth Fairhurst dead. Pickard's defence counsel, Mr Waddy, told the court that there was simply no evidence to put before the jury that proved that his client had committed the offence. He agreed with the common belief that the injury might have been caused by her falling down the steps. The judge told the jury that they had to decide whether the prisoner had committed the offence, and in what state of mind he had been at the time. If they felt that he had inflicted the wound without premeditation, then they must reduce the charge to that of manslaughter. Members of the jury were undecided and in the end found Jesse Pickard not guilty.

Before the prisoner was discharged Mr Justice Honyman criticized the way in which the clerk to the Barnsley magistrates had dealt with the statements that had been taken from the witnesses at the inquest. The judge claimed that the whole case for the prosecution had rested on the evidence of witnesses who had contradicted what they had previously said in their depositions. He warned the court that he fully intended to take the matter up with the Lord Chancellor about the manner in which the depositions had been taken and the way in which the case had been managed at Barnsley. He particularly mentioned the evidence of Mrs Beechill, which was so contrary, and that the deposition might have been written on 'waste paper' for all the good it had been. He told the jury that another case from Barnsley had been heard by him prior to the case against Jesse Pickard and there were discrepancies in those depositions also. He had considered sending for the clerk of the Barnsley magistrates during the trial, as the statements had changed so much from when they had first been taken down. Justice Honyman stated:

> It was a frightful state of things that a man's life might have been sacrificed simply from the depositions being wrongly taken, and that I feel thankful that I have never been tried for anything done in Yorkshire. The sooner that the attention of the country was [*sic*] called to the state of things the better. Whether it was the fault of the system or the individual I do not know, but anything more likely to defeat the ends of justice, I could not imagine than what went on in that part of the country.

He told the jury that he was fully intending to communicate with the magistrates at Barnsley and bring the matter to their attention. The prisoner was then discharged and he left the courtroom. At that point only he knew whether he had actually got away with the murder of Elizabeth Fairhurst.

CHAPTER EIGHT

A Determined Attack by a Rejected Suitor

One of the cases that Mr Justice Honyman had referred to in the trial of Jesse Packard was that of a stabbing, which had also taken place in Barnsley in June 1873. A few months earlier, a single woman called Mary Pavor had come to live with her sister and brother-in-law at Brunswick Place, Dodworth Road, Barnsley. Prior to moving in with her sister she had been keeping company with a young man called Thomas Green, aged thirty-five, who came from Brierley, a small village about 6 miles from Barnsley. Mary herself had been born at Brierley, and it was there that the couple had met and became engaged. This lasted until Green enlisted in the Royal Marines in 1872. A few months later, in August, for some unknown reason Mary informed Green that she had changed her mind and did not wish to see him again. He sent her many letters begging her to reconsider, but she always refused. On being discharged from the Marines in March 1873, Green returned to Barnsley, where he continued to pester Mary to become engaged once more. A newspaper report on the case stated that, finding his entreaties useless, he then threatened

Map of Brierley, where Mary Pavor met Thomas Green.

to kill her, 'declaring that if she did not marry him he would make her so that she could marry no one else'. Even when he found employment as a labourer in Barnsley he would follow Mary about the town, and several people had witnessed him threatening her. However, she continued to refuse to have him back and matters quickly deteriorated. Thomas Green had apparently informed many of his acquaintances that 'if she would not have him, he would take care she was not in a state to marry anyone else'.

On the night of 18 June 1873, at about 8.45 pm Mary was returning home from work and was walking along Dodworth Road when she saw Green approaching. To her evident relief he walked straight past her without speaking, although he muttered something that Mary did not hear. She continued walking and when she got to about 40 yards away from the house where she lived with her sister and brother-in-law, Mary again heard Green call out to her. A newspaper reported that he asked her 'if she had changed her mind and would take him back again', and Mary had told him in no uncertain terms that 'she would never keep company with him again, and that, furthermore, she wanted him to stay away from her'. He then asked her if she would go for a little walk with him, but again Mary refused. As she had by now reached the gate to the yard where she lived, she turned to go up the path. Out of the corner of her eye Mary saw Green run at her. She turned her head and was horrified to see him lifting a heavy 'cane-stick' into the air and he began to beat her savagely over the head with it. Mary was knocked to the ground as her attacker continued to rain blows on her. Mustering all her strength Mary managed to pull herself to her feet and ran towards the safety of the door of the house.

Green's training in the Marines had stood him in good stead and he pursued her and dragged her once more to the ground. The now terrified girl felt him bending over her and, staring at her former lover, she saw him take out a large sailor's clasp knife. Opening the blade, and with a swiftness that she could hardly believe, Mary felt Green cut at her throat two or three times. She felt the blood flow from her neck and, with what strength she could she muster, she called out 'Murder!' at the top of her voice. A married woman called Mrs Mary Eliza Monsel lived in the house next door to the victim's sister. Hearing the girl shout out, she came to the door of her own house, where she saw the two people struggling on the ground. Mrs Monsel bravely attempted to pull Green off the girl as she seized the cane-stick, which Green had put down to the side of him. She proceeded to beat the attacker over the back, as she called out, 'Help, help, he is killing her.'

Thankfully, at that time, Barnsley surgeon Mr John Blackburn was proceeding along Dodworth Road in a gig, when he saw the attack being carried out. He immediately leapt to the ground and grabbed the attacker by the wrist, and shook it until the knife fell out of his hand. The surgeon tried to pull him away from the girl, but Green doggedly fought him off. The way in which Dr Blackburn finally subdued Green was by grabbing him by the throat and pushing him onto his back, throttling him at the same time. Dr Blackburn then managed to get hold of the knife, which he put in his own pocket. By now the girl was almost insensible from the loss of blood, and Dr Blackburn immediately went to her assistance. A group of people who had been attracted by the scuffle carried Mary carefully into her sister's house and placed her on a sofa. They then seized Green and held onto him while the police were sent for. With the prisoner now being held safely, Dr Blackburn, along with his colleagues Doctors Smith and Morris, who had also been attracted by the screams, attended to Mary's wounds.

PC Neil, of Barnsley, arrived and took possession of the bloody knife and the cane-stick, which he noted had been weighted at one end with lead. Green was escorted through the streets of the town to the police station. He was described as being 'a big powerful man with a very determined look'. Nevertheless, when he arrived at the station the only regret he expressed was that he hadn't managed to kill Mary Pavor. Meanwhile, Mr Blackburn found that the wound in the girl's throat was triangular in shape. It was a very deep wound, about 1½ inches in length. It was very near to the carotid artery and if it had been a bit longer, Mary would most certainly have bled to death. He also noticed that there was extensive bruising along the girl's throat and chin. Dr Blackburn stitched up her throat, but Mary had already lost so much blood that it was thought she would soon die. In the event, later that same evening a magistrate went to the house to take what was thought to be Mary's last dying deposition. Only afterwards did Dr Blackburn find that his own coat and waistcoat had been cut through in two places on the right breast. Although he hadn't felt it at the time, he now realized that he had been in great danger himself.

On Friday, 20 June 1873, Thomas Green was brought up in front of the magistrates at Barnsley Town Hall charged with attempted murder. The case had caused a lot of excitement, and as a consequence the court itself was very full. Mary was described by the local newspapers as being 'a respectably connected young woman'. Superintendent Sykes asked for a remand for the prisoner on the grounds that Mary was still in a delicate state and unable to attend to give evidence. A remand was granted until the following Monday. When the court reconvened, people outside watched in silence as the young girl arrived at the courthouse in a cab. She was accompanied by a nurse, who assisted her into the courtroom, and then she sat to give her evidence. Superintendent Sykes went over the scene for the magistrates, and he produced the jacket that the girl had been wearing at the time of the attack. The blood stains were still clearly visible on the material. PC Neil produced the knife, which had been given to him at the time by Dr Blackburn. When asked if he had anything to say, Green simply shook his head, seemingly unable to take in the scene before him. The jury found him guilty and he was ordered to take his trial at the next assizes. Green was taken to a cell at Leeds to await his trial.

Thomas Green was brought before the judge, Mr Justice Honyman, at Leeds Town Hall on Monday, 4 August 1873, charged with attempted murder. Green had no defence and so the judge asked Mr Wheelhouse to watch the case on the prisoner's behalf. Mr Wilberforce outlined the case for the prosecution and described the events of 18 June. According to a newspaper report, Green's defence, Mr Wheelhouse, stated that he could not deny that 'it was his client's hands that had inflicted the injuries'. In yet another case of a change to a previous statement, which would have been grimly noted by the judge, Green claimed that he had not intended to attack Mary Pavor. Mr Wheelhouse stated that Green was drunk at the time

A cell door underneath the Leeds Assizes.

he committed the act, and therefore was not responsible for his actions. He said that the prisoner had told him that he had committed the offence 'in such a passion that he was unable to control himself'. Mr Wheelhouse claimed that as a consequence, when Mary Pavor passed him in the street and did not speak, Green felt a huge surge of bitter resentment towards her, and had attacked her without thinking.

Despite his eloquent defence, the jury heard how Green had told anyone who would listen that he intended to revenge himself on the woman who had spurned his advances. They found Thomas Green not guilty of attempted murder, but guilty of the lesser offence of 'wounding with intent to do grievous bodily harm'. Mr Justice Honyman stated that, in his opinion, the jury had taken a very lenient view of the case and the prisoner had had a very narrow escape. Had they found him guilty of attempted murder, he would have considered it his duty to send him to prison for the rest of his life. Reports stated he concluded that 'the claims of justice would not be met adequately unless he passed the most severe sentence that was within his power'. He then sentenced Thomas Green to twelve years' penal servitude for the attack on his former sweetheart.

CHAPTER NINE

Death at the Albert Dining Rooms

Amost serious poisoning case was reported in Barnsley in September 1878, which panicked the whole town and put Barnsley on the national map. It started in the most innocuous way when eight victims fell ill after eating some poisoned bread and butter pudding at an eating house. It was called the Albert Dining Rooms, and was situated on Sheffield Road, Barnsley. The eating house had been opened about six months previously and its hours of business were from 8.00 am to 9.00 pm every day of the week. It was owned by Mr William Thresh. He was a Barnsley auctioneer and a married man who lived with his wife Emma and six children at their house further along Sheffield Road. As their eldest daughter had been confined to bed with an illness for three months, to devote as much time as possible to the invalid Mrs Thresh usually

Sheffield Road, where the Albert Dining Rooms were situated.

ordered meals from the dining rooms to be sent to the house. The menu at the eating house was designed by William and the cook. A servant girl named Letty Heppenstall also helped out in the kitchen. Mr Thresh had recently sacked the previous cook, a woman called Eliza Martin, as he maintained that she was dishonest. He had appointed the new cook, Mary Ann Rhodes, who started work on Monday, 9 September 1878.

Matters had progressed in an ordinary fashion and William Thresh had no reason to complain about the new cook until two days later, on the morning of Wednesday, 11 September. The night before, William had ordered two bread and butter puddings to be made – a large one and a smaller one. Mary Ann Rhodes made the two puddings the same day and she cooked the largest pudding in a Dutch oven, and the smaller one in an oven in a separate part of the kitchen. The Dutch oven was in a room partitioned off from the dining rooms themselves. The fires for both ovens had been lit by the manager of the dining rooms, Henry Mason, whose niece was the same Letty Heppenstall who helped out in the kitchen. The puddings were in the ovens for approximately an hour and a half before Mary Ann took the one from the Dutch oven out first, which seemed to be nicely cooked. At about noon she placed them both on the kitchen table at the dining rooms. When the puddings had cooled, William told Mary Ann to send the largest pudding to his house. The cook gave it to a boy called Emmanuel Cherry, with instructions to take it to Mr Thresh's house. The boy carried the pudding, which was wrapped in a clean towel, and handed it to a maid. The smaller pudding was placed for sale in the dining rooms' window.

A man called Thomas Thawley, a miner from Thurgoland, was shopping in Barnsley with his wife on that same day. After completing their shopping the couple decided they would eat at the Albert Dining Rooms, where they arrived a little before 1.00 pm. They both had some mutton and potatoes but after eating this meal Thomas remarked to his wife that he did not feel satisfied and asked Mr Thresh if he had some pudding for sale. William Thresh indicated the bread pudding that was still in the window, and Thomas agreed that he would like a portion. He was given some of the pudding and ate it with relish, but by the time he was walking home he had begun to feel very ill. When he arrived at Dodworth he felt a stinging pain in his insides and about a mile from home he began to be sick at the side of the road and noted that the vomit was green in colour.

At the house on Sheffield Road, Mrs Thresh noticed the pudding at teatime when her daughter Ann, aged fourteen, said that she had tasted it and it seemed as if it was 'going sour'. Mrs Thresh tried a piece, but thought that it tasted alright, and as a consequence her other five children all had some with their tea. No one seemed to be poorly until about 8.00 pm when Mrs Thresh put the children to bed as normal. They all became ill after they had been in bed just a short while. When William came home at about 9.30 pm he too was feeling sick, and told his wife that he had eaten some of the bread and butter pudding at the shop and thought that it had disagreed with him. To their increasing horror, all of the family was stricken with sickness and diarrhoea, which became increasingly worse throughout the very long night. First thing in the morning, surgeon Mr William Stewart was sent for. Mr and Mrs Thresh told him that they thought they had been poisoned by some bread and butter pudding that they had eaten the previous day. The surgeon examined the remains of the pudding, which he smelled and thought was very sour. When Mr Stewart went into the parlour he saw the youngest daughter, 3-year-old Emma, on the sofa. He examined the little girl and found that not only was she suffering from diarrhoea and sickness, but she also had a very high temperature. He did what he could for the family, but when he left William was still very ill, as were two servants and Ann, who had complained about the taste of the pudding to her mother.

Mr Stewart returned later that day and although he had treated the patients all in the same way, he noticed that Emma had quickly become insensible. Disturbed at this point, he thought that she was exhibiting symptoms of congestion of the brain. He called on a colleague, Dr Lancaster, to discuss the case with him, and he agreed to accompany him to the house if he needed to visit the family again. Mr Stewart was called out in the middle of the night to attend to Emma, who had got increasingly worse, and he arrived with Mr Lancaster. The two men did what they could for the child, but she died at

6.40 am on the Friday morning. To their increasing concern they also attended to the other patients, who were by now all becoming insensible and exhibiting the same symptoms of congestion of the brain. During the morning William's brother John arrived after being told of the family's illness. Mr Thresh instructed him to go to the shop and destroy any of the bread and butter pudding that remained. When John returned back to his brother's house he told the family the news that other people who had eaten the pudding were also dangerously ill. William was told that his manager, Henry Mason, aged fifty-two, had been taken very ill about half an hour after eating the pudding, and he was in a very poor state.

An inquest was held for Emma Thresh on Saturday, 14 September 1878 at the Coach and Horses Hotel, Barnsley, by coroner Mr J. Taylor. Surgeon William Stewart told the inquest that he was a member of the Royal College of Physicians and had known the deceased all her life, as he had attended the mother at her birth. He said that the whole of the Thresh family were still confined to bed, and although he told the coroner that they were feeling better, they were still unable to give evidence at the inquest. He added that of all the family, the daughter Ann was much better, and he had high hopes of her complete recovery. Mr Stewart described the symptoms and how he had treated Emma. He then told the coroner that he had conducted a post-mortem on the body of Emma Thresh on Friday night with Dr Lancaster and another surgeon, Mr James Stewart. On opening the abdomen they had found about a spoonful of a thick yellow substance. The small intestine was very inflamed and the kidneys were congested. The surgeon described how he had examined the other organs, which were mainly healthy. He gave the opinion that the cause of death was inflammation of the stomach, intestines and the brain, which could only be produced by the introduction of some irritant poison. The coroner asked Mr Stewart what they thought that might be, and he told him that all the symptoms were compatible with the administration of arsenical poison. He added that they suspected that the poison had been added to the bread and butter pudding. The inquest was then adjourned in order that the family might recover and be able to give evidence themselves.

The following week, Mrs Emma Thresh was well enough to attend the court and she stated that the pudding in question had been brought to the house, and she described how after eating some of the pudding everyone, including the servants, took ill. The coroner, who was obviously looking for a motive, asked her if there was anyone at the eating house that had shown any ill will towards them as a family. Mrs Thresh simply shook her head and told him that she did not know of anyone. The servant at the eating house, Letty Heppenstall, told the inquest that she had nothing to do with the cooking for the rest of the week, apart from on a Sunday, when it was the cook's day off. Usually she was only responsible for serving the food and washing up. Letty stated to the inquest that in the past, the food had been cooked by the former cook, Eliza Martin. The new cook was a woman called Mary Ann Rhodes, who had just recently been employed. On the Tuesday when William asked for the two bread and butter puddings to be made, Letty had seen Mary Ann Rhodes bring in some two-day old crusts of bread. She watched as the woman left them to soak in water all night in an earthenware dish for use on the following day. Letty described how there was not enough bread with the crusts, and so Mary Ann sliced open another loaf and added that to make sufficient for two puddings.

Letty continued with her evidence and said that on the Wednesday she was eating her dinner at the shop, when her uncle, the manager Henry Mason, entered. He saw what she was eating and he cut himself a slice. He had eaten some of the pudding, but commented that it did not taste the same 'as if it was made at home'. She later found out that another pudding had been sent to William Thresh's house. Problems with vermin in any kitchen were often eradicated by the use of vermin killers that contained arsenic. The coroner therefore asked her if she had ever seen any mice at the dining rooms, or knew of any vermin powder that might have been used. She told him that although there were mice in the eating house, she did not know of any vermin powder being used around the place. John Thresh stated that on the Thursday morning he had been called up by a waiter from the shop, a man called Thomas Whitfield. He had told him that all members of his brother's family were ill. As instructed by his brother he had

gone to the Albert Dining Rooms, but could not find any
of the second pudding that was supposed to have been left.
Letty Heppenstall was recalled and she stated that she too had
looked for the second pudding, but there was no sign of it,
or the dish that had contained it, anywhere in the kitchen. A
day or so later, both William and John Thresh were both at the
dining rooms and they made a thorough search for the missing
pudding. They eventually found the remains in a swill bin at
the back of the kitchen. At that point the coroner told the court
that he intended to close the enquiry until the remains of the
pudding, the stomach of the victim and samples of vomit could
be analyzed. He informed the inquest that they were to be sent
to Mr Allen, the public analyst, and that the inquest was to be
adjourned while they awaited his report.

The town of Barnsley was alive with the reports of the
poisoning at the Albert Dining Rooms. By the next day, Sunday,
15 September, reporters were descending on the area and were
anxious to cover the story. Surgeon Mr Stewart, who was then
attending Mr Henry Mason, was interviewed, and he told a
reporter that the man was so ill that he was unconscious and
he doubted very much that he would recover. The surgeon
said that William Thresh and his eldest son were also very ill,
and he thought that inflammation had set in. He stated that
leeches had been applied to both father and son, and as a
consequence they seemed a little easier. It was also reported
that Mary Ann Rhodes, who had made the pudding, was also
very ill. On Monday, 16 September, another man was listed
as being ill from the same source. Mr Thomas Thawley had
dined at the eating rooms and although he ate some of the
bread and butter pudding, his wife had refused it. His wife told
reporters that while they were in the shop another woman had
gone in and purchased some of the pudding, which she took
away in a basin. When they arrived home on the Wednesday,
she assumed that her husband's illness was something else, for
which he had been treated by his own surgeon. When the stories
about the poisoning had circulated, a message had been sent to
Barnsley to contact Mr Stewart, who was treating William and
his family. He immediately went to see Mr Thawley and found
him exhibiting the same symptoms as the others. Mrs Thawley

reported that her husband was still in a very weak state and still suffering from sickness and diarrhoea.

By the following day, Tuesday, 17 September, there was an update that gave slightly better news. It was reported that the Thresh family were recovering very slowly, and they were now able to sit up and eat normally. Mary Ann Rhodes was said to be feeling much better and Thomas Thawley was also recovering well, although Henry Mason was still in a very critical state. Despite their improved condition, the next day news was heard that Henry Mason had died, and another inquest was arranged by the coroner, Mr J. Taylor. It was held once again at the Coach and Horses Hotel, Barnsley, in the evening of Thursday, 19 September. Mrs Mason was the first to give evidence, and she stated that when they both left home on the morning of 11 September her husband had seemed to be quite well. He was taken ill on his return that night, and quickly became unconscious on the Friday, and remained so up to his death at 2.00 pm on the following Wednesday. A surgeon, James O'Connell, stated that he had attended Mr Mason on the morning of 13 September. He complained of vomiting copiously and of having an intense thirst. The surgeon saw how his whole body was convulsing. The following day, Mr Mason seemed a little better, but was still unconscious and unable to talk. He remained the same over the next few days and was still in a coma when he died. Earlier that day Mr O'Connell had completed a post-mortem with Dr Stewart, and they had found that inside the stomach, there was about 6 ounces of a yellowish-brown fluid. They had both concluded that his death had been caused by the introduction of some irritant poison. A portion of the viscera belonging to the dead man had been sent away for analysis, and the inquest was then adjourned until the return of the analyst's report. It was sadly reported that Mr Mason left a widow and several children.

Rumours about the cause of the poisoning were discussed freely in the local newspapers of the time, as reporters desperately searched for the reason behind the deaths. Some accounts said that copper pans, which had been used in the cooking, might have been the instruments of the poisoning. It was suggested that just a few grains of copper would produce the symptoms described. Others blamed it on the fact that the bread that had been used had been 'sour' and the ingredients when they had been examined appeared to be putrefying and fermenting. Others still blamed it on the fact that the bread had been two or three days old when it was used as an ingredient for the puddings. Many of the inhabitants of the town, the legal authorities and the newspaper reporters hoped that the analysis of the remains of the little girl Emma Thresh and Henry Mason might throw some light onto the reasons for the mysterious deaths.

The inquest was opened again at the Coach and Horses on Thursday, 26 September. On this occasion the cook, Mary Ann Rhodes, was able to appear to give evidence. She told the coroner that she had been employed as a cook at the dining rooms by Mr Thresh. She started work on Monday, 9 September, and explained that she had been accustomed to cooking and would regularly cook all the food that was required for the menus for the next three days. Mary Ann was instructed on Tuesday, 10 September to steep some bread that night in order that two bread and butter puddings could be made the following day. She was told to make one large and the second small, but when William told her to make the two puddings, he had not told her which one was to be sent to his house. Mary Ann told the inquest that she was handed the bread by a waiter, Thomas Whitfield. He had got the bread from the side of the counter. The cook described how she had checked the bread and found it to be a little dry but not mouldy, and had left it to steep all night in a brown bowl. In the morning, after the milk had been delivered at 10.00 am, she squeezed the water out of the bread. She poured a quart of milk and four eggs into the pudding before adding half a pound of coarse sugar. William had told her to go easy on the currants, so she only added about a quarter of a pound, before finishing it off with nutmeg. This mixture she stirred carefully before pouring the contents into two earthenware bowls. She described how she had cooked the larger of the two puddings in the Dutch oven, adding that she also cooked meat in the same Dutch oven and no one complained of the meat.

Mary Ann Rhodes was asked by a member of the jury if there had been any disputes in the kitchen in the days before the poisonings. She told him that as far as she could recall there had not been an argument between any of the staff in the kitchen, or in the eating house. Mary Ann said that she had some of the pudding, and she had served William and another customer who she now knew was Mr Thomas Thawley with the pudding. She described how she lifted it out of the dish with an ordinary, common metal spoon that had been in the kitchen all the time she had worked there. She added that the spoons were always removed after serving. Mary Ann then described her own symptoms, stating that she had not felt ill straight away after eating the pudding and had not felt ill until she returned home in the evening.

The other man who had been poisoned now also attended the inquest. Thomas Thawley gave evidence that when he had been ill on the Wednesday he returned home and called in his local doctor the following day. Dr Blackwell, after hearing of his condition, treated him for English cholera. It was only after a friend called to see him on the Sunday night and asked him if he had had any bread pudding at the Albert Dining Rooms that he realized he had been poisoned. The coroner thanked him for his evidence and congratulated him on his recovery. He was followed by Mr William Thresh, who gave evidence that his daughter Emma had been a delicate child from birth. There had been so many rumours about the previous cook, Emily Martin, that he was asked by the coroner if she had returned back to the premises after she had been sacked. He told him that she had come into the shop on Sunday, 8 September to collect some of her things, but only stayed for about fifteen minutes and he had not seen her since.

Sergeant Brown gave evidence that he had received samples from Dr Stewart in glass jars and had taken them to the borough analyst, Mr Alfred Allen in Sheffield, on Monday, 16 September. The analyst then introduced himself and gave his credentials. He stated that he was a consulting chemist of Surrey Street, Sheffield, the public analyst for the West Riding of Yorkshire and a lecturer in chemistry to the Sheffield School of Medicine. He told the court how he had examined the samples for several poisons and found none. Most appallingly, Mr Allen described how he had also given a 6-week-old puppy some of the pudding, and that he had 'thrived on it'. He admitted that the puppy had been sick but, as young puppies often do, he had eaten the vomit with no ill effects. On testing half a pound of the second pudding, however, the analyst had found minute quantities of lead, zinc and even smaller quantities of copper. These minute deposits were less than one twentieth of a grain. Mr Allen described how he had tested samples from the stomach of Emma Thresh, but had found no trace of poison in the remains. He suggested that the only thing left was to carry out further tests on more samples, and he told the coroner that he still had to test the liver from Henry Mason. He placed the blame for the failure to detect any poison on the fact that fresh vomit had not been saved earlier. This might have still contained some residue of the poison, if there had been any. The coroner pointed out the significance of finding the reasons for the poisonings and then stated that the matter had become one of national importance. He added that if the Secretary of State was to be communicated with, he might help the legal authorities in Barnsley with the matter of expenses. He agreed that the facts of the case would be forwarded to him for his decision, and the inquest was then adjourned.

It was announced at the next inquest, on Thursday, 10 October, that a letter dated 28 September had been received by the coroner from the Home Secretary at Whitehall. The letter expressed thanks to the coroner for applying for authority to make further analysis in the case of Henry Mason and Emma Thresh, and concluded:

> I am to request that you send samples of the pudding to this office with a view to further analysis being made. I am at the same time to enquire whether the stomachs and intestines of the deceased persons above mentioned, who died after eating the pudding, are in a condition to admit to a second analysis.

The letter was signed Mr Geoffrey Lushington. Mr Allen then attended and told the coroner that he had continued with his examinations of the samples, but had found nothing. He said that he had researched some cases of eating mouldy bread that had proved poisonous. He quoted a case in which horses had died within a very short space of time after ingesting such mouldy bread. He then went into a long explanation of fungi and mould. Mr Allen stated that in his tests he had found that a substance called 'ergot' had been found to be poisonous, but he had failed to detect any in the samples. He concluded that the pudding had contained some substance that had resembled ergot, which would be the only conclusion that could account for the effects that had been observed. Mr Allen said that Mr Thawley had stated that the bread and butter pudding was 'sloppy'. This suggested to him that it had not been properly cooked and therefore he thought that 'sour food' was the cause. Doctors Stewart and Connelly gave their evidence, which agreed with Mr Allen's assumptions.

Finally, the two bakers that regularly delivered bread to the premises, John Robinson, of Grace Street, and William Hanger, a delivery man for John Robinson, then gave evidence. They both stated that the bread they had supplied had always been freshly baked. They confirmed that on some occasions the bread was newly baked and still warm from the ovens when it was delivered to the Albert Dining Rooms on Sheffield Road. Despite their assertions, what happened to the bread once it had arrived at the eating house could not be so easily dispelled. Superintendent Sykes told the coroner that he had visited the shop on several occasions and had seen crusts of bread 'laying about'. The jury retired and returned after ten minutes with the following verdict:

> The jury is of the opinion that the deceased Emma Thresh and Henry Mason came to their deaths from eating a portion of a certain unwholesome pudding; but how or by what means such pudding became unwholesome, there is not sufficient evidence to show.

There was certainly a strong suspicion at the time that the disgruntled cook had managed to slip some arsenic into the bread when she visited the shop on the Sunday before the poisonings. Yet there had been no complaints of illness before the Wednesday, when other people and members of the Thresh family were taken ill. Several eminent analysts from Birmingham,

Glasgow, Liverpool and Dublin offered their opinions as to the causes of the Barnsley poisonings. They all suggested that death was a result of some kind of fungus or rancid food. Mr Stewart, the surgeon involved in treating the patients and the man in the best position to know, also offered his suggestions. He quoted an eminent work on fungal poisoning undertaken by a German doctor called Van Boeck that he had studied, and concluded that the cause of the poisonings must be put down to mouldy bread. The reality of it is that two people died, but whether from deliberate or accidental poisonings, from this distance of time we will never really know.

Chapter Ten

Murdered by a 14-year-old Stepbrother

Resarch shows that there are many cases of murder or manslaughter that are the result of a situation exacerbated when one or more of the parties involved have been drinking. Imagined slights take on enormous importance under the influence of alcohol, and when this is mixed with a loaded gun and a young boy of fourteen, the outcome can be deadly. On Sunday, 27 December 1874, a man called George Jessop met up with his brother Henry and the pair went drinking in Wombwell, which is about 4 miles from Barnsley. The two brothers went to the Traveller's Rest Inn, where they stayed until about 9.00 pm. They then called in at the Ship Inn before leaving at 10.00 pm to meet up with their father, Joseph, and their stepmother, Ellen, at a house nearby. Joseph and Ellen had

The Traveller's Rest Inn, now derelict, where George and Henry Jessop were drinking before Henry was killed.

been with friends named Mr and Mrs Birkinshaw all day, with a son of Ellen's from a previous marriage, George Skefferton. Throughout the day, the party had been drinking more or less continuously, and when George and Henry arrived there was some banter exchanged. At some point Henry had attempted to kiss Mrs Birkinshaw under the mistletoe, and it was then that Joseph Jessop told his family it was time to go.

Joseph was a prosperous and industrious man who made his living working at the Lundhill Colliery. He was reported to be a 'steady' man who had lost his first wife, after a marriage lasting ten years, in a tragic drowning three years previously at Wombwell Junction. By the time he returned home with his sons and his wife and stepson it was around 11.00 pm, and there they found the youngest stepson, John Henry Skefferton, who was aged fourteen. The adults continued drinking and were all a bit the worse for wear. Seated in the kitchen Joseph complained to Henry about his attempted misbehavior with Mrs Birkinshaw, and Henry told him it was all in fun and challenged Joseph to a wrestling match. This was quite a common occurrence in this boisterous family, particularly between Joseph and Henry after they had been drinking. Newspaper reports state that Henry jokingly told his father that 'he was getting too long in the tooth' and that 'he could easily throw him if he wanted to'. Joseph accepted the challenge and by the light of the fire the two men began to wrestle. At some point Mrs Jessop noticed that the atmosphere had changed, and she tried to separate the two men as they began to wrestle in earnest. While she was trying to pull Henry off his father, he kicked her accidentally in the leg. Still under the influence of alcohol and seemingly affronted by Henry's attack, Ellen went in search of a policeman, but she was unable to find one.

It seems that in her absence John Henry was also alarmed at the seriousness of the men's struggling, which no longer appeared to be the game it had started as, and he ran upstairs. When he came back into the kitchen he was holding a pistol. No one could quite recall how it happened, but there was the sound of a gun going off and Henry Jessop slumped to the floor covered in blood. Joseph could not believe what his young stepson had done as he looked up and saw him still holding the gun. Young

John Henry seemed to be as stunned as the other men in the house. He had apparently gone into the bedroom where the gun had been kept and, assuming it was unloaded, had grabbed the pistol and inserted a cap that would allow the gun to be fired. He had only intended to frighten the two men enough to stop them from fighting in the hope that his mother would bring back a policeman. He had not realized that the gun had been loaded with powder, and as a result he had shot his stepbrother. Meanwhile, Ellen, unable to find a policeman, called into the house of a neighbour called William Hanks and asked him to come back to the house with her. She was telling him how the play fight had got out of hand, when they approached the passage leading to the house. There she met George Jessop, who told her that his brother had been killed. She ran into the house and found the deceased lying on the kitchen floor, covered in blood. In a sudden panic she ran into another room, to where her young son John Henry followed her. He was crying, and saying that he had not meant to hurt Henry, but that his pistol had 'just gone off'. He gave her the gun, which she threw into the fireplace. Later, realizing that she could not get rid of the gun so easily, and while the other occupants were waiting for the surgeon, she took the gun out of the fire and concealed it in the privy.

Dr John Nelson Miller was sent for, but when he arrived he found that Henry Jessop was dead. There was a serious wound on his right temple, where the bullet had entered the brain. About half an hour later, Police Constable Jonas Taylor, of Wombwell, arrived. He was joined soon after by Inspector William Edmund Corden, of Barnsley Police. They searched the house and found the small pistol concealed in the privy nearby. George, his father, Joseph, and John Henry Skefferton were taken to Barnsley Police Station. When the young man was charged with causing the death of the deceased by shooting him with a pistol, he told the officer:

I went upstairs and got the pistol from underneath the mattress. I took a cap out of my waistcoat pocket, and put it on and went downstairs and shot at them, thinking just to frighten them.

He was also accused of burying the pistol in the privy. The young prisoner was crying when he stated that he had not buried the gun but his mother had taken it from him and hidden it. On Monday morning, 28 December, the three prisoners appeared before the magistrates, where George Skefferton and Joseph Jessop were released. John Henry was remanded for a further week, charged with the murder of his stepbrother.

On Wednesday, 30 December, an inquest was heard for Henry Jessop at the Ship Inn, Wombwell, before the coroner, D. Wightman Esquire. The prisoner, looking very young and afraid, was escorted into the court by Inspector Corden. He was defended by Mr F. Parker Rhodes, a Rotherham solicitor. The coroner opened the proceedings and stated to the jury that they had to decide how the deceased man had met with his death. The prisoner's mother, Ellen, was the first to give evidence. She described the day's events and how the party left the Birkinshaw's at about 11.00 pm and returned home. She told the court how Henry had challenged his father to a wrestling match and how she had been kicked. In answer to a question from a juryman she told him that neither of her sons

The Magistrates' Court, where John Henry Skefferton appeared.

or stepsons had ever quarreled with their father or each other. On the contrary, she said that they had always been 'on the best of terms with each other'.

The next witness was her husband, who told the coroner that in the middle of the scuffling he heard the sound of 'a crack like a whip', but he did not see any flash. He was holding his son and just felt his body go limp. He thought he was play-acting, and roughly told him to go home to his house, as he lived nearby. Only then did he notice the blood on his son and realized that he was dead. He told the coroner that he was aware that there had been two pistols in the house, and that he had ordered Henry to get rid of both of them. He stated that he remembered a conversation with his son from earlier in the year, when Henry had told him that he had sold both guns. George Jessop gave evidence that he had gone to the pub with Henry, and described the 'lark' of attempting to kiss Mrs Birkinshaw under the mistletoe. Back at the house, he had seen his stepbrother, John Henry, run upstairs while the two men were wrestling on the floor, but thought nothing of it. Only when John Henry returned and he then saw a flash did he realize what had happened. To his horror, he then saw the blood coming from the wound on his brother's head. There had been no light in the room, only the light of the fire in the grate. Consequently, the room was too dark to see any details, and that was why he had only seen the flash. George told the coroner that he had loaded the pistol a week before Christmas, when he was planning to go out shooting. When the shooting had been cancelled, he had forgotten that the gun was loaded. He too agreed that there had been no quarrel between any members of the family, and that they had all got on well together.

Neighbour William Hanks described going into the kitchen and seeing the dead body. Mr Parker Rhodes asked him how well he could see in the kitchen. He told him that the room was full of smoke, and was only lit by the fire, which was at that point dying down. Police Constable Taylor stated that at about 11.30 pm on the Sunday night, he heard that 'someone had been shot at the Jessop house'. He went to the house, where he found that George Jessop was 'the worse for wear for drink'. When he entered the house he found George laid over the body of his brother, crying and saying, 'My brother has been shot'. PC Taylor told the coroner that George was in a terrible state and had to be forcibly removed from the body. The constable searched the house and found a shot bag and powder flask in the bedroom. These items were produced and shown to the jury. On searching the young lad John Henry, he found nine caps in his waistcoat pocket. Inspector Corden stated that he had found the pistol buried in excreta in the outside privy, but he was unable to determine whether it had been recently fired or not. The surgeon, Mr Miller, described the wound on the deceased man as being 'large and rugged', about an inch above his right ear. Later, when he undertook the post-mortem, he found that there were fragments of bone embedded in the skull. He gave his opinion that in consequence of the serious nature of the wound, death would have been instantaneous.

The coroner, Mr Wightman, summed up the evidence, stating:

> In my opinion, the prisoner's statement to the police constable confirmed the most important part of the evidence. He was the only sober person amongst the party and the statement made by him had placed you in a much better position than juries generally are on such enquiries. It is now your duty to consider the whole of the facts and return such a verdict as you think proper.

He told the jury that they had to decide whether the boy had intended to shoot his stepbrother, or whether he had only intended to frighten him. If they thought it was the latter, then it would be manslaughter with no malicious intent involved. However, if they felt that the firing of the pistol was intended to injure the deceased, but not actually kill him, they must return a verdict of wilful murder. After an absence of three quarters of an hour, the jury returned to court, where they found the prisoner John Henry Skefferton guilty of wilful murder. The coroner stated that he agreed with the verdict and could not see how the jury could have come to any other conclusion. At the end of the inquest, which had lasted over four hours, John Henry Skefferton was sent to take his trial at the West Riding

Assizes. It was noted that the young man did not show any sign of understanding of the seriousness of his position as he was led out of the inquest room still accompanied by Inspector Cordon.

On Monday, 4 January 1875, John Henry was brought before the magistrates at Barnsley Town Hall, where he was once again defended by Mr Parker Rhodes. The evidence heard was the same as that at the coroner's inquest, with the exception of a plan of the rooms in the house, which had been made by surveyor Mr John Robinson. The plan included the rooms and the passage, as well as the outbuildings. Once again, the case lasted for five hours, and the prisoner was found guilty. Under advice from Mr Parker Rhodes, he reserved his defence. John Henry Skefferton was now fifteen years of age when he appeared before the judge, Baron Amphlett, at the assizes at

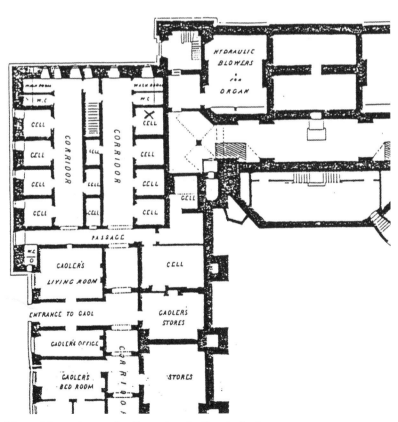

Map of the prisoners' cells under the Leeds Assizes.

Leeds on Friday, 2 April 1875. He was brought out of the cells beneath the courtroom and placed in the dock. The prosecution made out that Joseph Jessop had angrily tried to remonstrate with his sons, and as a result the old man had been 'thrown to the ground'. He described how John Henry had shot at Henry Jessop, who had been lying on top of his father. The prosecution claimed that the young man was fond of playing with the pistol, and was in the habit of keeping caps in his waistcoat pocket. The defence counsel, Mr Foster, stated that the pistol had belonged to George Jessop and John Henry did not know the gun was loaded. He pointed out that the young prisoner had always claimed that he simply wanted to frighten Henry Jessop into leaving his stepfather alone. His stepfather, Joseph Jessop, also stated that his sons were used to the wrestling matches, and that Henry had 'pulled him about' rather than thrown him to the ground, as had been suggested. But the main issue of the case rested on the fact of whether or not John Henry knew whether the gun was loaded. George Jessop told the judge that he had loaded the pistol with powder on 18 December, but that he didn't put a cap in it.

Mr Foster concluded by repeating that John Henry had not known that the pistol was loaded, and therefore there was no case to answer. He pointed out that there was more of a case of culpability for George Jessop, for being 'stupid enough to load a pistol and leave it for anyone to make use of'. The judge in summing up stated that the jury must be clear in their mind whether the prisoner knew that the gun was loaded when he fired the weapon. However, he could be guilty of 'culpable neglect' if he did not check to see if the gun was loaded, and in that case it would be a charge of manslaughter. The jury agreed and found John Henry Skefferton guilty of manslaughter, and asked for a recommendation for mercy because of his youth. The judge told the prisoner:

I think the jury has come to the right conclusion because it was no doubt an act of culpable negligence, in that you made use of the pistol in the way you have, without being perfectly certain that the pistol was unloaded. I believe myself on the whole that you, though you did not make any enquiry upon the subject, I entirely believe that you did not suspect it was loaded; and you certainly during that evening appeared to act the part of a good son, because you were not intoxicated and you attempted to save your stepfather from the violence of his own sons.

He then imposed a very lenient sentence on John Henry, 'in the hope that he had learned his lesson regarding the use of firearms'. He told him that he would be imprisoned for a week and as the assizes had already been open now for more than seven days, he was allowed to go free. There was little doubt that the boy would have learned his lesson as there had seemed to be no disagreement within the family in the past. Undoubtedly, the experience would have made him more wary of handling guns in the future.

CHAPTER ELEVEN

Child Murder in Barnsley

In the nineteenth century, women in Britain who had a child out of wedlock were usually shunned by so-called 'respectable society'. Almost without exception, the woman was blamed, and the man usually escaped scot-free. If she was abandoned by her parents, the woman sometimes had no option but to throw herself on the mercy of strangers. Desperate women were driven to conceal the fact that they were pregnant for nine months, and then had to somehow dispose of the baby in whatever way they could when it was born. As a result, the numbers of dead babies found in pits, rivers and canals were phenomenal throughout Britain, and in this, Barnsley was no different. Legal measures were put in place to deal with such women, but little thought or consideration was given to the psychological effects that having to commit such a deed would have upon them.

By May 1867, the crime was becoming so common in Barnsley that when the body of yet another baby was found, on Friday, 16 May, it was commented in the local newspaper that, 'There have been five or six similar cases of exposure in the neighbourhood during the last twelve months.' Such cases were difficult to prove, and so when another little body was found, at Worsbrough Dale on 16 April 1872 at 4.00 pm, yet another inquest was arranged. The child had been found by an underground labourer named John Yates, who had seen the body floating in the Dearne and Dove Canal. With the assistance of a man called Millward, he got the body out and took it to the nearby Mason's Arms. They then gave information to the police at Barnsley. An inquest was held, where the jury heard that the surgeon, Dr Wainwright, had undertaken the post-mortem. He stated that the child had been recently born and it had air in the lungs, so he concluded that it had led a separate existence from its mother. Dr Wainwright gave his opinion that 'the child had died from suffocation in the water' and the jury returned a verdict of 'murdered by drowning by some person or persons unknown'.

Police enquiries soon established that a 19-year-old girl called Sarah Elizabeth Longbottom was suspected of recently having given birth. On Thursday, 18 April 1872, she was interviewed and arrested by PC Dewhurst on a charge of concealing the birth. At first Sarah denied the charge, despite the fact that the baby had been found only 300 or 400 yards from where she lived with her mother. Sarah was still denying the charge when she appeared before the Barnsley magistrates on Friday, 19 April 1872, where she was remanded until the following Monday. There appeared to be some sympathy for the girl in the local press, as she was described as a 'respectably dressed young woman'. However, when she appeared again, the situation had completely changed. Sergeant Forrest, of the Barnsley Police, told the court that on Sunday, 21 April, the defendant had told him she wanted to make a confession, and she then made the following statement, which he read out:

> I want to tell you that I have taken that child that was drowned in the canal. I am sorry I did so. I threw it in myself. I did not hear it breathe and I believed it was dead.

After her confession, PC Dewhurst had returned back to Sarah's mother's house to establish whether or not she had bought any baby clothes or made any preparation for the birth. The fact that she had not indicated her guilt and the charge was now changed to one of murder.

Ann Oliver, the wife of a grocer of Worsbrough Dale, told the magistrates that she had known the prisoner for four months, as she frequently called in at her shop. She had noted that the girl looked pregnant, but did not say anything to her about it. By 16 April, her shape had changed so much that Mrs Oliver felt bound to ask Sarah if she had been ill. Sarah told her that she had not been eating and she had been suffering from dropsy. After hearing from other witnesses who also had suspected that the girl was pregnant, the magistrates found her guilty and she was committed to take her trial at the assizes. On Tuesday,

Map of Worsbrough Dale, where
Sarah Elizabeth Longbottom
was found guilty of murdering
her newly born child.

6 August 1872, Sarah Elizabeth Longbottom was brought
before the judge, Baron Cleasby, at Leeds Assizes on the charge
of wilful murder. Thankfully, she was defended by Mr Vernon
Blackburn, who advised her to plead guilty to the lesser charge
of concealment of birth, which she did. The judge, in summing
up, told her:

> You had not only concealed the birth of your child, but you also
> denied the fact of your pregnancy, attributing your physical
> appearance to dropsy. By a mere accident the body of the
> child was found shortly after the birth. When you found that
> concealment would no longer avail, you finally acknowledged
> that you had given birth to an infant.

Baron Cleasby then sentenced her to nine months' imprisonment.
Prison sentences for women were very hard in the nineteenth
century, and even when she was released it would have been
difficult for her to return back to anything like a normal life. But
in some respects Sarah was lucky; other women were sentenced
to death.

On Monday, 11 August 1884, the body of a female child
aged about five weeks was found in a pool of water. The
pool was around 200 yards away from the footpath situated
between Locke Park and Stainborough, and about 2½ miles
from Barnsley. The body was discovered by a schoolboy named
William Kaye, aged twelve, who had the presence of mind
to take the child's body to the police station. It was handed

Locke Park, near where another baby's body was found.

over to Police Constable George Dale, who was stationed at Stainborough. PC Dale accompanied the boy, who showed him where the body of the child had been found, and he noted that the pool was almost hidden by a bush. PC Dale took the child to the Stratford Arms in order that it might be identified, and gave it to the landlady, Mary Ann Boothroyd. Elizabeth Hurst, an elderly woman who lived near the Stratford Arms, was called in to wash and lay out the little child's body. She undressed the child and saw that there were no obvious signs of injury. Its face was much swollen, but was still pleasant to look at.

As the news of the finding of the body spread, many people from the area came to the Stratford Arms to see the child, which was finally identified by a woman called Mrs Mary Ann Hawksworth. She saw the clothes that the baby had been wearing and knew immediately who the mother was. The widow told the police that on 2 July a girl called Ann Parkin had appeared at her door at Grace Street, Barnsley, in great distress as her labour pains had started. Mrs Hawksworth admitted that she had taken pity on the young woman, and later that same night a baby was born. The girl told Mrs Hawksworth that she was a domestic servant aged twenty-five, and that her parents lived at Dodworth Bottom, but they had refused to have her at home because of the 'misfortune' that had befallen her. Her benefactor looked after Ann during her confinement, and had also found some clothes to take the baby away in. Mrs Hawksworth noted that the girl had appeared 'extremely low and depressed' throughout her stay. A neighbour named Ann Kenworthy, who had visited the house during Ann's stay, also concluded that the girl had been in poor spirits after the birth. She was described as 'a very quiet patient and did not speak unless she was spoken to'.

Mrs Hawksworth told the police that the girl had remained at her house for five weeks, before leaving at 11.15 am on 5 August. She said that the child had been dressed in the same clothing in which it had been found and it had also been covered in a shawl. When Ann left, taking the baby with her, she told Mrs Hawksworth that she was going to Silkstone to see some relatives there. Later that same day, Ann Parkin arrived at the home of her brother, James, and sister-in-law, Eliza, at Dodworth. She arrived at about 10.30 pm and was wearing the shawl, but she had no baby with her. She stayed at the house with James and his wife for nine days and during that time she did not mention the baby once. Eliza Parkin knew that her husband had always been very fond of his sister, and that she had often turned to him in times of trouble.

Meanwhile, PC Dale immediately started to make enquiries in the local area for any woman that had been pregnant, or had been suspected of being pregnant, and the name of Ann Parkin was given to him. Detective Sergeant William Lodge, of Barnsley, spoke about arresting the girl on 10 August at her brother's house. When arrested Ann denied having given birth to any child. The baby was buried two days after this. Ann Parkin was brought before the magistrates at the Police Courts at Barnsley on Friday, 15 August 1884. PC Dale showed the jury some of the clothes that the child had been wearing at the time it was found, which had been identified by Mrs Hawksworth. After hearing the evidence Ann Parkin was charged with the murder of her illegitimate child. The case had caused considerable excitement in the area, and large crowds turned out in order to see the young woman. The magistrates, Mr F.H. Taylor and Mr R. Inns, heard the evidence of Mrs Hawksworth and it was noted that throughout the short enquiry that Ann appeared to feel her position very keenly, and was quite distraught. Her parents, who were described as 'respectable, working-class' people, were also in the courtroom as she was brought in. At that point Superintendent Kane offered no evidence against her as he explained that enquiries were still ongoing, and Ann was simply remanded. The following week, on Friday, 22 August, Ann was once more brought into court, where she was undefended. A solicitor, Mr J. Carrington, prosecuted on behalf of the Treasury. He stated that an order had been received from the Secretary of State that very morning, requesting that the body of the baby be exhumed. He asked that a post-mortem examination should be carried out to ascertain the cause of death. As a consequence, a further remand was given to the following Monday.

When the court reconvened, the first witness was the sexton of the church, James Hemingway, who gave evidence of the burial of the child's body and its exhumation on 22 August. Police surgeon Dr Blackburn told the court that he had carried out the post-mortem and that the child had not died from drowning as he had at first believed. The post-mortem revealed that the child's skull had been fractured in eight places. He stated that this was an incredible amount of violence for it to have been subjected to during its short life. In answer to a question from the magistrates, Dr Blackburn gave his opinion that either the child had more than one fall, or several blows had been inflicted on its head before it had died. In his opinion the cause of death was concussion of the brain. Sergeant Kane stated that Ann had said that when she left Mrs Hawksworth's house she had dropped the baby on a piece of grass. Dr Blackburn was recalled but he said that would not have caused several injuries. The sergeant also told the court that the prisoner had been in a very despondent frame of mind since her incarceration. Sergeant William Lodge gave evidence about the arrest at Dodworth and when charged with the crime, the prisoner had given another version of events. She had said to him, 'I did not kill it; I was going over the fields to Stainborough. I missed my way and fell into the water with my child and lost it.' Despite her statement

The judge's chair, Leeds Assizes, where Baron Pollock sentenced Sarah to death.

of innocence the prisoner was found guilty and sent to take her trial.

Ann Parkin appeared at the assizes at York Castle on Monday, 17 November 1884 in front of the judge, Baron Pollock, charged of the murder of her child. Thankfully on this occasion she was defended by Mr Vernon Blackburn. On opening the case for the prosecution, Mr Gerald Hardy described the kindness of Mrs Hawksworth, who had taken the girl into her house and cared for her while she gave birth. He said that the prisoner had remained in the house for five weeks, and during that time the baby was in very good health. Mr Hardy said that she left the house on Grace Street to go to her brother's house, where she stayed with him and his wife for nine days. During that time she did not mention the baby once. He suggested to the jury that she had battered the child's head before throwing it into the water.

William Kaye, the 12-year-old boy who had found the baby, was the next to give evidence. He stated that he and some friends had been playing in the pool, where they usually went to bathe. He was in the water when he saw a bundle, which turned out to be the baby, about a yard from the bank. The water at that place was about 3½ feet deep. The boys got the bundle out using long sticks. William stated that the face of the baby was discoloured and there was some clay on the face, which he wiped off before giving it to PC Dale.

Herbert Crawshaw's evidence was next. He told the court that he was an architect and surveyor and had been asked to measure the pool indicated to him by PC Dale. Mr Crawshaw said that the pool was about 16 feet wide and 3½ feet deep. The soil near to where the body had been found was a clayey type mixed with gravel, and there was no fencing around the pool.

Mr Hardy then told the court that this closed the case for the prosecution. The defence's case for Ann Parkin was short as he called no witnesses. Finally, Mr Hardy summed up for the jury. He questioned Ann's evidence and asked why she had not attempted to get the body out of the pool after having fallen in. Thankfully, the defence, Mr Vernon Blackburn, showed more ability in his summing up than he had in presenting the witnesses. He claimed that the prosecution's case was made up of nothing more than probabilities, possibilities and suggestions. He stated:

> The facts are that on the way the prisoner missed her footing near to the pool, which was not fenced in. She claimed that she fell into the water with the child, and in struggling to save herself, she lost hold of the child, which was fatally injured in the water. When she arrived at her brother's house at Dodworth, she was alone. No one mentioned the child and nothing more was heard of it until the body was found.

Mr Blackburn pointed out that the prisoner had not made any mention of the baby at her brother's house, not because she felt guilty about giving birth to an illegitimate baby, but because she was friendless and alone. He made little of the evidence of Mrs Hawksworth and Mrs Kenworthy as to the birth and subsequent identification of the clothing worn by the dead child. However, he emphasized that it was clear from the two women's statements that the circumstances around the birth had left the prisoner unhinged in her mind, and she was probably still in that state when she dropped the body. Mr Blackburn also pointed out that the child's body had been buried for sixteen days before exhumation and that the injuries to the skull could well have been due to the fact that it had deteriorated during that time. He claimed that the prosecution's suggestion that Ann had battered the baby was wrong, and that the injuries were more likely to have been caused by her falling onto the baby as they both plunged into the water. He urged the jury that if they felt any doubt at all about the prisoner's account, they were to give her the benefit of that doubt and discharge her.

The judge also summed up for the jury. He noted that no one had actually witnessed the girl and child falling into the water, and therefore it was only the prisoner's word that she had. He warned the jury that they could not dismiss her confession even though she had no intention of killing the child. In such circumstances the charge would have to be reduced to one of manslaughter. The jury retired and after an absence of only twenty minutes returned with a verdict of guilty of murder, with a strong recommendation for mercy. Ann, who had been seated

The Goaler's Journal, in which the governor listed all sentences and reprieves.

throughout the trial and was by now pale and trembling, stood up, with the assistance of a female warder, as the judge gave her the sentence of death. Placing on his head the black cap he told her:

> Ann Parkin, you have been found guilty of the crime of wilful murder and it is my duty to pass upon you the sentence of the law which necessarily follows upon such a verdict. I do not think that any words of mine could be of use either with regard to the public ... or yourself, except to remind you that I do hope that during such time as will remain to you here, you use that time in looking for pardon and for peace, where peace and pardon can be found.

Ann was taken out of the court in a fainting condition. Thankfully, on Friday, 21 November 1884, the High Sheriff of York received an official communication from the Home Secretary, which he directed to the governor of York Castle Prison. The letter stated that the carrying out of the sentence of death on Ann Parkin was to be respited until Her Majesty's further pleasure be known. Her sentence was later commuted to life imprisonment.

CHAPTER TWELVE

Death at Measborough Dike

Killiam Teale's father and grandfather moved to the Ardsley area of Barnsley in 1851, when they were both employed as contractors for the South Yorkshire Railway when the branch line was built from Doncaster to Barnsley. Teale had always been a sickly child who was afflicted with more than his share of childhood diseases, and as a result of this had spent a lot of time in bed. Consequently, he did not walk until he was about five years of age. Throughout his life he had also suffered several bouts of rheumatism, which had affected him so badly that on occasions he was unable to move about or get out of bed. As he grew into adulthood, Teale became a little stronger, and by 1867 he was employed at the office of Messrs Cammell and Co, of the New Oaks Colliery as a clerk. He had worked there for ten years and part of his

New Oaks Colliery.

job involved collecting the rents of cottages owned by the firm. Teale was also employed as the secretary to the Ardsley Working Men's Conservative Club. His childhood illnesses, his slight stature and nervous nature made him a figure of fun for some of the lads who worked at the New Oaks Colliery and others who lived in the district around Measborough Dike. His journey home to Ardsley would take him through Measborough Dike and some boys were in the habit of waylaying and taunting him. As a result he made sure to avoid the area on his way back and forth to his work at Barnsley.

By June of 1887, Teale was described as a timid man who was generally quiet and inoffensive when he was sober. However, like many timid men, his demeanor changed after he had been drinking. On 25 June 1887, there was a cricket match held at Ardsley, which had been attended by Teale, now aged thirty, and some of his friends. After the match the group went into Barnsley, where they visited several public houses before heading home along Doncaster Road about 11.00 pm. It was said that Teale was quite intoxicated as he went home with his friends. One of the men, named Woodward, was engaged in the ginger pop trade, and as a result his nickname among the gang of lads was 'Poppy'. As is often the way, although the nickname was used freely between them, the men were liable to take exception to other people using it. That night they hadn't gone very far before they were joined by a group of young boys. One of them was called John William Clarke, and as he passed Woodward, in fun he shouted out: 'Pop, pop'.

This so annoyed Teale that he ran after Clarke and struck him so hard across his head that he began to cry. A newspaper report states that another boy in the group, Ernest Walton, told him, 'You will not have it all your own way when you get to the dike,' and Teale retorted that 'he was ready for all of them'. Two of the boys, John Clarke and Herbert Brown, ran off in the direction of Measborough Dike. When they reached the Pinder Oaks Hotel, John Clarke was still very upset and crying. He complained to another young man called John Taylor, aged nineteen, and told him that he had been attacked for something that was only meant to be a joke. Just then, William Teale's group approached, and Clarke pointed out the man who had struck him. Taylor went up to Teale and, grabbing both his arms, asked him what he had done to the boy. Whether in rage or fear, he could never afterwards say, but Teale pulled a pocketknife out and, almost immediately, blood gushed from Taylor's neck onto the road. Taylor cried out, 'Fetch a doctor, I have been stabbed.' He then managed to walk about 50 yards towards the Pinder Oaks Hotel, where he lived with his grandfather, before falling down. Meanwhile, Teale attempted to run away, but he had only got about 150 yards before he was captured and taken into the pub. He was there ten minutes later, when Taylor died.

The nearest surgeon, Dr McMillan, was called, but when he arrived he found that the young man was already dead. He examined him and saw that the jugular vein had been cut through, on the right side of his neck. A woman called Mary Hinchcliffe, who had seen the attack, saw Inspector Birkinshaw and Police Constable Gaythorpe on duty at the Sheffield Road, and told them that a man had been murdered. By the time they returned to the scene, a crowd had gathered outside the Pinder Oaks Hotel and the two policemen had difficulty in protecting Teale against the mob, which was out for his blood. It seems that John Taylor had been a very popular young man, and the crowd would have lynched his attacker without hesitation. The grandfather of the deceased boy also appeared and was terribly distraught at the death of his grandson. He too joined in with the crowd as they attempted to attack Teale. It was only with the greatest difficulty that he was extracted from the crowd and arrested. Teale was returned to Barnsley and locked in a cell at Westgate Police Station charged with the murder of John Taylor.

The police later returned to the scene and found the knife that had been used in the attack was in the possession of a man called Richard Hollier, who had picked it up. The knife was a large one and was still smeared with the blood of the victim. When it was shown to the prisoner, he identified it as his own. It was described as a double-bladed knife with a corkscrew, bottle opener and other implements attached to the handle. Police enquiries continued, but witnesses were unable to state whether Teale had drawn the knife out of his pocket, or if it was already in his hand when John grabbed his arms. The attack caused such a sensation that over the next few days hundreds of people visited the site at Measborough Dike and the Pinder Oaks Hotel. What most people could not understand was the fact that, prior to the attack, both men had been described as respectable, honest men. Up to that point Teale had always presented as a nervous, quiet individual, so it could not be guessed what had driven him to commit murder. John Taylor was known to be a responsible, steady youth, who a fortnight previously had won a knurr and spell competition and had been presented with a prize of £20 – a considerable sum in those days. Knurr and spell is a traditional game in which a 'knurr' (ball) is hit by a 'spell' (a bat), the object being to hit the ball as far as possible.

On Monday, 27 June 1887, William Teale was brought before the magistrates, Messrs F.H. Taylor, R. Inns and E. Lancaster, at Barnsley, charged with wilful murder. When he entered the courtroom, people were struck by the way in which he seemed to be looking about him in a strange, excited way. Although he appeared to be listening carefully, he did not display any understanding of the desperateness of his plight. The local newspaper noted his timidity and stated that he was:

> an insignificant looking man, short in stature with somewhat wizened features, and small fishy eyes. When brought into court, he was evidently labouring under great excitement, and he gazed first at the bench, then at the police, and finally at the spectators with quite a frightened look.

Teale was defended by Mr W.E. Raley, and Mr J. Carrington prosecuted. Superintendent Kane went over the details of the case and told the court how Teale had stabbed John Taylor without any provocation. One of the magistrates, Mr Taylor, asked the superintendent if Teale had the chance to open the knife before the attack began, but the superintendent told him that he didn't have time. He told the magistrates that the witnesses confirmed that 'there was no time between when Taylor put his hands on his arms, and his being stabbed'. The conclusion was that the knife was already opened in his hand. The superintendent asked for a remand of eight days, which was granted, and Teale was removed to the cells. The prisoner seemed pleased when the case, short though it was, came to an end and he was able to escape from the sight of all those people in the courtroom.

On Monday, 4 July, Teale appeared once more before the magistrates. He seemed much calmer than he had been on his previous appearance and was allowed to sit during the proceedings. Mr Carrington opened the case and told the jury:

> The facts as I should present them were sad in the extreme, and I admit of a twofold sympathy – first with a sympathy to the parents and friends of the prisoner; and secondly a sympathy with the parents and relations of the unfortunate man, who was now no more.

John William Clarke told the court how Teale had chased him and boxed his ears. He described the attack on John Taylor and stated that he too did not see the knife in the prisoner's hand. He had simply witnessed the blood coming from the deceased man's neck. Other evidence was heard before the court broke for lunch. After the court had returned, two miners, Harry Ellis and John Henry Holle, of Measborough Dike, stated that they had witnessed the stabbing. They saw Taylor as he held both of Teale's arms, then they saw the prisoner get his right arm loose and watched in horror as he struck at Taylor with the knife. Inspector Birkinshaw stated that when he took the prisoner into custody and charged him with 'causing the death of John Taylor', Teale told him, 'I am innocent.' In summing up, Mr Carrington stated that he could not deny that the attack had taken place, but spoke of the great provocation offered to his client and reminded the jury of his previous good character. Nevertheless, the jury found William Teale guilty of the manslaughter of John Taylor, and the bench committed him for trial. He was allowed bail, with two sureties of £50 each.

On Tuesday, 2 August 1887, William Teale was brought before Mr Justice Mathew at the assizes at Leeds Town Hall, where he pleaded not guilty. Mr Milvain prosecuted, and Mr C. Mellor defended Teale. The first witness was the boy John William Clark, who admitted that the prisoner was the worse for drink when he struck him. Mary Hinchcliffe told the judge that she had seen the knife in Teale's hand when she saw him

The courtroom at Leeds Assizes.

striking Clark. She had heard him wave the knife at the boy and mutter something about being 'quite prepared for them at Measborough Dike'. His defence, Mr Mellor, stated that 'he had not the least doubt that the boys intended to wait for Teale to give him a severe thrashing at Measborough Dike, over a harmless bit of name calling.' He said, 'If it hadn't been for Taylor accosting him, Teale would have gone on his way without any further ado.' He claimed that the prisoner had merely acted out of self-defence, and it was not impossible for him to have forgotten that he had an open knife in his hand at the time of the attack.

The judge summed up for the jury and told them:

The evidence would not justify the charge against the prisoner that he intended to take the life of the deceased. You would probably take the view that what was done was done wrongly, but that it was done with no intent or expectation that the wound would turn out to be a deadly one. That by no means exonerates the prisoner from the charge of manslaughter, although I am clearly of the opinion that he never meant to inflict even a serious injury upon the deceased man. If he unlawfully wounded him and in consequence of that wound caused his death, he, apart from any intent, is guilty of manslaughter.

After a short consultation, the jury found William Teale guilty, but added a plea for mercy on account of the provocation he had received. Sentence was deferred to the following day. On the next day, the judge in sentencing him told him that he understood he might have been alarmed for his personal safety, but the foolishness of having a knife on his person could not be ignored. He added that he hoped Teale would keep away from public houses and control his temper in the future. He then sentenced him to three months' imprisonment with hard labour.

CHAPTER THIRTEEN

The Monk Bretton Murder

Monk Bretton is a peaceful little village that has been occupied since medieval times, and is the site of Monk Bretton Priory, established in 1154. It is situated about 2 miles from Barnsley town centre. It has always been noted for being a quiet, restful place and so there remains quite a mystery as to why, in the nineteenth century, it became the place where two murders took place. The first was committed by a man named Mr William Henry Emeris Burke in February 1888. At that time he was a 42-year-old surgeon with a very successful practice at Monk Bretton. He was also employed as the colliery surgeon for both the Monkton Main and Carlton Main collieries, a position he had held for the last ten years. Burke lived in the Manor House in the village with his wife, Katherine Jane, the daughter of The Reverend A. Lambert. As a consequence William Burke was well known to the inhabitants of the area and the people of the surrounding districts, being thought of as having a genial temperament and kindly nature. It would seem that this pleasant, middle-class doctor had it all; so how did he become embroiled in a murder that would rock the nation and cause questions to be asked in Parliament?

It seems that the happy married life the couple had enjoyed was marred due to the doctor's addiction to alcohol. On several occasions his wife had left him for this reason and gone to stay with her sister, who was married to The Reverend J. Longley, of Grimesthorpe Vicarage, near Grimsby. Each time she had taken with her the couple's two children, a little girl, Aileen Ethel Dona, born 1879, and a son, name unknown, born 1886. After a short while Burke would attempt reconciliation, promising to change, and she would agree to take him back, and they would return to their married life at Monk Bretton. The latest reconciliation had just taken place, in January 1888, when Mrs Burke agreed once again to try to make the marriage work. On her return, however, she was soon made aware that during her absence her husband had indulged freely in alcohol while his professional work had been attended to by a locum. The doctor had promised to change if his wife returned to him, and for a while he endeavoured to pull himself together.

They were both feeling that matters were improving when they attended a ball at Barnsley on 2 February 1888, but on their return home Burke told Katherine that he had to go out again, and she saw no more of him that night. His addiction was not helped by the close proximity to the Manor House of the nearby Norman Inn. It was a favourite drinking place for the doctor and he could often be found there chatting to the landlord, George Taylor, and other local men. On Saturday, 4 February 1888, he had been at the inn since noon, and at 6.00 pm he asked for a pen and some notepaper, which George Taylor supplied. Burke told George that he wanted to write a letter to his wife, but the landlord noted no difference in his behaviour. He remained in the public house until returning home around 8.30 pm, when Burke persuaded his wife to go to Barnsley that evening with him in their carriage. When she asked where they were going,

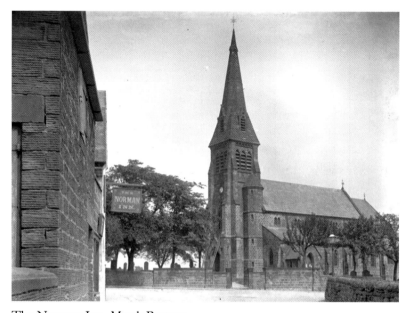

The Norman Inn, Monk Bretton.

he told her that they were going to take their beloved daughter, Aileen, whom he called 'Topsy Chatterbox', to see a pantomime. At that time Aileen was in bed, but somehow he urged his wife to wake her up and dress her in order that she might go with them to the theatre at Barnsley. Reluctantly the three of them entered the pony and trap, which had been waiting outside the house, Burke's excited daughter sitting beside him. However, the trap had only gone a few hundred yards when it pulled up outside the Norman Inn and they all went inside. Burke called for some champagne, which his wife paid for.

They sat down in what was described as the inn's best room, where the doctor proceeded to drink all the champagne himself. What transpired between the couple in the next two hours was unknown, but at 10.55 pm, Mrs Burke ran out of the room screaming at the top of her voice. Police Constable Francis Emsley, the local constable, was in the habit of calling in at the inn to make sure that it closed on time. He was in the passage when Mrs Burke told him, 'The doctor has a revolver,' and urged the constable to 'take it from him'. PC Emsley was approaching the door of the room when he heard a shot fired, and as he opened the door he saw little Aileen fall onto the hearthrug. He then saw Dr Burke walk across the room and fire the gun into his own breast, falling back into a chair as he said, 'I've missed.' PC Emsley went immediately to the child and attempted to pick her up, but he found that she was already dead from the wound in the left side of her chest. Meanwhile, the landlord, having heard the disturbance, rushed into the room along with other patrons of the inn.

A message was sent to Barnsley for Dr Saddler, who quickly appeared on the scene. He saw Dr Burke seated on a long settle, apparently asleep. After confirming that Aileen Burke was indeed dead, Dr Sadler went to his colleague and he saw immediately that the wound was not fatal. Burke was removed to the Beckett Hospital and Dispensary in Barnsley, where, shortly after noon the following day, a bullet was extracted from his chest. In all the time he was in hospital, Burke never spoke to anyone about what had happened in the room at the pub that night, or what had caused him to shoot the daughter he loved so dearly. A police constable remained at the hospital with him. Meanwhile,

Beckett Hospital, Barnsley.

Beckett Hospital and Dispensary.

Superintendent Kane and Inspector Gunn had proceeded in a waggonette to the Norman Inn. They told the landlord that they had orders to make a thorough search of the room. They found the gun, which was identified as a six-chambered revolver, with four of the bullets still left inside.

On Monday, 6 February 1888, an inquest was held at the Norman Inn for the dead child. The case had caused such a sensation in the area that there was quite a crowd waiting outside the inn at the appointed time, but if they hoped to see the

A typical pistol of the period.

prisoner they were disappointed, as he remained in the hospital. Solicitor John Carrington had been instructed to watch the case on behalf of his client, Dr Burke. The Beckett Hospital doctor stated that although Dr Burke was still at the hospital, his wound was not a serious one and there was every hope for his survival. The chief witness at the inquest was, of course, Mrs Katherine Jane Burke. She described how her husband had returned home on the night of the murder and against her wishes wanted to take the child to a pantomime in Barnsley. The little boy had wanted to go too, but his father told him that he was to stay at home. She described how most reluctantly she had taken the sleeping child out of bed and they had gone to the Norman Inn.

Mrs Burke then described how she could see that her husband was intending staying at the inn, and so eventually she went into the other room and asked the village blacksmith to take the trap back to the Manor House. He agreed, and she returned back to the room where her husband and child remained. She stated that her husband seemed very excited and was talking wildly, which she put down to the alcohol he had consumed. Then she noticed Burke putting his hand into his pocket and, to her horror, saw him pull out a gun. She assumed that he was going to shoot her, and so she screamed and ran out of the room as quickly as she could to get help. Mrs Burke saw PC Emsley and entreated him to take the gun away from her husband. Then she heard the first shot, followed by a second, and entering the room with the constable, she saw her daughter Aileen on the floor. Dr Saddler told the coroner that the bullet had passed through the little girl's heart and lungs, causing immediate death. He said that Dr Burke must have stood over her and placed the gun against her chest to shoot her. Consequently, there was a lot of blood spilled, whereas the wound to Dr Burke seemed only superficial and hardly bled at all.

PC Emsley identified a letter that had also been found in the room. He told the coroner that Dr Burke had pointed to the letter and had attempted to pick it up, but Mrs Burke got there first, saw it was addressed to herself and put it into her pocket. Later, after her husband's arrest, she handed the letter to Superintendent Kane. While waiting for medical help to arrive, Dr Burke had asked for the dead child to be brought to him, and he kissed the little girl gently. The body of the child was then removed to her home and placed on the bed from which she had so recently been taken. The coroner summed up for the jury, and a verdict of wilful murder was given against Dr Burke. The body of Aileen Burke was interred the following day. On Saturday, 10 March 1888, a message was received by Superintendent Kane to say that Burke was in a fit state to be removed from the hospital. Superintendent Kane was waiting outside the ward and the doctor was arrested. They arranged for him to be taken before the magistrates at the West Riding Court at Barnsley the following morning and charged with the murder of his daughter. However, on the morning he was due to appear, the police surgeon Dr Blackburn judged that the weather was too cold, and due to the injuries that the doctor had sustained, it was agreed he would not attend. Two solicitors were present at the magistrates' court in his absence, and the court agreed to put off the case until Tuesday, 27 March.

When Dr Burke was finally brought into court he looked extremely pale and was given a chair to sit in while hearing the evidence against him. Mr Williams, of Wakefield, acted as the prosecution, and the prisoner was defended by Mr Charles Mellor. Mr Williams opened the proceedings and stated that

Insignia of West Riding Courthouse.

from the evidence brought before them it was clear that Dr Burke had shot the child and fully intended to take his own life. When it came to the crucial evidence of the letter written by Burke, there was disappointment in the court when Mr Williams stated that he was not going to read the letter out. He merely pointed out that it was written in a reasonably grammatical style, was punctuated correctly and gave the impression of being written by a person who was absolutely in his right mind. Mrs Burke repeated the statement that she had made at the inquest of the night's events. George Taylor, the landlord of the Norman Inn, then gave his evidence and he told the magistrate that Dr Burke was in the regular habit of visiting his house. He said that on the day of the murder the prisoner had left the house about 8.30 pm and returned an hour later accompanied by his wife and daughter. Mr Williams then brought the court's attention back to the letter. He asked the magistrates to allow the letter to be read, but Dr Burke's solicitor, Mr Mellor, objected. He stated that as a wife, Mrs Burke should not have been called to give evidence against her husband in the first place. He pointed out that the letter had been addressed to her and should not be read out. Despite all his protests, the bench felt that it was crucial to the case and ordered that the letter should be read out.

The letter was addressed to 'Kitty Burke, Monk Bretton', and contrary to Mr Williams' pronouncement it seems disjointed and irrational, revealing the doctor's probable state of mind. The letter also reveals the possible motive behind the couple's unhappy marriage and the reason for his excessive drinking. Dated 4 February 1888, it stated:

My wife Kitty,

At one time I loved you hard, but you have completely converted this into entire indifference by your actions, in that several times you ran away from me and left me. I now adore Mary, alias Mary Ann Taylor, née Woodcock. She has, for the sake of her children, discarded me, asking if I may say it, that this should be as clandestine as it was before. To this, after importunity and entreaty I begged to decline.

Now bid me goodbye, Kit.

W.H.E. Burke

AD [addendum] Today have had one glass of sparkling Burgundy of our own, one and a half bottles of *vin ordinaire* [claret] and four two penny worth of scotch whisky. This is all I have had to drink.

PS Kitty, may I write one word more, and that is, I know you loved me truly, but you threw my love.

Despite the implications that the letter was clearly intended as a 'goodbye' to his wife, Mr Mellor concluded the defence's case by suggesting that the revolver was fired accidentally. He suggested that, appalled at what had happened, Burke then attempted to commit suicide. The magistrates deliberated and the prisoner was found guilty and was committed for trial. Many people felt disappointed at the outcome and felt that the committal had resulted in more questions than answers. Mainly they wanted to know why a respectable doctor would shoot the very child that he professed to love.

The *Leeds Mercury* summed up the general feeling about the case on 8 February 1888, when it attempted to appoint a reason for the purposeless crime:

> It was surely a premeditated crime. It was the husband and father who had abandoned himself to despair … Dr Burke had simply given himself up to the curse of drink. He had sunk himself beyond redemption in his passion for drink, and in an evil moment when the balance of the brain was gone, he shot his pet child with more callousness than he would have shot his dog. Horrified at his crime, he attempted his own life, without success, and now awaits a doom which will brand his name for ever with the most shameful of all humiliations.

On Saturday, 5 May 1888, Dr Burke was brought before Mr Justice Mathew at the Leeds Assizes charged with the murder of his daughter. Mr West and Mr Harold Thomas conducted the case for the crown, and Mr Charles Mellor and Mr Barstow were for the defence. Significantly, Mr Whitaker Thompson watched the case on behalf of the woman mentioned in the letter, Mrs Mary Ann Taylor, although no other details about her were heard. Mr West outlined the case for the jury stating that due to his dissipation, Dr Burke had 'injured his health and constitution and impaired his moral sense'. He said that although the motive was unclear, that undoubtedly Dr Burke was in the habit of carrying with him a loaded revolver. Mr West said that whilst it was obvious that the doctor was unhappy, it was unclear why he decided to shoot his daughter. He told the jury that they had to decide whether it was a clear case of murder, unless the evidence indicated to them that it had been an accident, or was a case for insanity.

The landlord gave his evidence and a member of the jury asked him if he knew of a reason why the prisoner should constantly carry a loaded gun. He told the court that the area around Barnsley was particularly wild and dangerous for any night journeys that the doctor had to undertake. He also spoke of the great affection between the prisoner and his daughter, which he had witnessed on several previous occasions. Dr Blackburn gave evidence that the child had died instantaneously and would not have felt any pain. He also stated that he had observed the prisoner during his stay in the hospital, and had witnessed no signs of insanity. This closed the evidence for the prosecution. Mr Mellor then addressed the jury for the defence. He stated that there was simply no evidence of any motive for the crime. He pointed out that if Dr Burke had wished to kill his wife or his daughter, that he could have done it more effectively and secretively at home. Mr Mellor then came out with a possible reason for the murder. He claimed that as the constable entered the room, in panic, as Dr Burke was taking the pistol out of his pocket, it went off accidentally, killing the little girl. He disagreed that the letter was coherent and stated that it seemed to him to be written by a man 'sodden with drink'. No witnesses were called for the defence.

The judge summed up for the jury, telling them that if they thought the child had been killed accidentally, they must carefully weigh the evidence. There was little doubt that the child had been killed by her father's hand, and they had to decide on the veracity of the police constable's evidence. The jury retired and after fifty minutes returned to the court with a verdict of 'guilty'. His Lordship then placed the black cap on his head and passed the sentence of death on Dr Burke. He told the prisoner to stand, and as the doctor got to his feet he said to him that drunkenness was no excuse for murder. He said:

> You have been convicted by the jury on overwhelming evidence of the crime of wilful murder. You stand in that dock, an example where no such example was needed, of the awful effects of intemperance. You are a man, we are informed, of high education and great intelligence, but reduced for the time being by drinking to the level of the lowest and most worthless of human creatures. It is my most painful and most melancholy duty to pass upon you the sentence which the law prescribes for your offence.

The prisoner, who had been supported by two warders, was then removed from the court and afterwards taken in a cab to Armley Gaol.

It was not long before petitions were sent to the Secretary of State asking for a commutation of the sentence. The case was held up by the Temperance Movement as a prime example of where drunkenness could lead. In an appeal, which Dr Burke

Armley Gaol.

wrote himself, he claimed that he had been drinking heavily for some weeks before the murder, and that he was also suffering from exhaustion and mental depression. Another appeal on medical grounds was sent by his solicitor, Mr John Carrington, which included more than 9,000 signatures. Many who signed the petition were from the medical profession and were from places as diverse as Manchester, Oldham and Cambridge. This appeal stated that at that moment in time, it was their opinion that Dr Burke was very weak and ill and suffering from depression. His half-brother, The Reverend H.M. Kennedy, added his support for his brother, stating that he was suffering from depression when he committed the crime and that 'if he is hanged there will be, from lack of sufficient enquiry, a terrible miscarriage of justice.' The Reverend Kennedy stated categorically that his half-brother should have been locked up for his own safety a full two months before the event occurred. It was also revealed that as early as January 1887, Dr Burke had told a colleague, Dr Macaulay, of Leicestershire, that 'Were it not for his children's sake he would kill himself.' Several people in Monk Bretton, and other places, had known of his threats to take his own life and of his unhappy marriage. When it became known on Monday, 21 May 1888 that the Home Secretary had respited Dr Burke, there were cries of outrage in the national press.

It seems that the doctor's health had broken down while he was in prison. Almost immediately after being admitted to Armley Gaol he was sent to the prison infirmary suffering from the effects of the gunshot wound. The prison medical officer, Dr Hawkins, found that the shot on the left-hand side of his chest had begun to heal, but there was still plenty of discharge coming from the other wound. Not surprisingly, in November 1888 Dr William Burke was struck off the rolls of the Medical Council. Matters continued until, just a year later, on Monday, 25 November 1889, when his Barnsley solicitor, Mr Carrington, received notification that his client was due to be set free. The letter stated: 'Dr Burke will shortly be released from Parkhurst Prison on the Isle of Wight due to his very delicate health.' It seems that the wound he inflicted on himself ensured that both lungs had been seriously affected, and that he had been in the prison hospital for some time. However, before he could be released, the solicitor learned that he had died. An inquest was held at the prison on Friday, 29 November 1889, which stated that soon after his conviction Dr Burke was removed to the infirmary at Wormwood Scrubs. On 16 May 1889, he was removed to Parkhurst Prison to serve out the rest of his sentence. Once again, he was immediately detained in the hospital due to the effects of the gunshot wound, and that he had died that morning due to exhaustion. A telegram was sent to Mr Carrington to give him the information.

But it was the next murder committed in Barnsley in the same year that was inevitably compared to the murder committed by Dr Burke. The comparison threw the nation's press into a frenzy, and there were accusations that Dr Burke had received preferential treatment due to his superior status. Both were crimes of passion and both were committed with a similar six-chambered revolver, but there the similarity ended.

CHAPTER FOURTEEN

Murder of a Foreman

Messrs Chamberlain's brick and carbon factory on Dodworth Road, Barnsley, had been established for many years by 1888. The firm had started out just producing bricks, but when the manufacture of carbon for use in electric lighting became popular, the orders came flooding in and the factory expanded. Due to the expansion William Burridge, aged forty-seven, was appointed foreman of the department. He was reputed to be a hard worker who expected the men under him to work equally as hard. He was in charge of about twenty men and for much of his career he seemed to get on with them all fairly well. Burridge was a happily married man with four children, aged thirteen, eleven, six and two years, and lived with his wife on Eldon Terrace, Dodworth Road, Barnsley. He was rarely ill, but had not been very well for about a month

Dodworth Road.

before Wednesday, 21 March, when he reluctantly dragged himself out of bed to go to work. His wife begged him to stay at home, but he insisted on going in.

James William Richardson was aged twenty-three in the year 1888. He was said to be 'usually a quiet and respectable young man', but had been known to fly off into a passion on occasion. He had been employed as a labourer at Messrs Chamberlain's for five years, and he too was married, but there all resemblance between he and the foreman ended. Richardson had been married for two years. He and his wife had a daughter and were living with his father at Kingstone Place, Barnsley. His father was very well respected in the neighbourhood and was employed as a gardener by a West Riding justice of the peace. On Wednesday, 21 March, Richardson started his shift at the usual time of 5.30 am, and at 7.00 am was hard at work when the foreman, William Burridge, found fault with him. When Burridge told him off, he made some reply that resulted in him being sacked for insubordination. At first Richardson seemed to take the dismissal in his stride, as he simply walked out of the factory and went home to his father's house. Saying very little to his wife or his father, he washed himself and changed his shirt. He had breakfast with them both before leaving the house at 11.30 am, as he told his wife, to pick up the wages that were owed him and to 'finish up'. But did revenge burn in his soul?

Richardson went towards the office to pick up his wages and through a glass partition he could see Burridge talking to Mr Frank Chamberlain, the superintendent of the works. He remained outside the office until Burridge came out. The foreman ignored the younger man, whom he had just sacked, but he had only walked a few paces towards the carbon department when Richardson drew a revolver and shot him. He fired three

Kingstone Place.

or four shots into Burridge as he fell and lay on the floor. Frank Chamberlain looked up, horrified, and saw Richardson with his arm outstretched as he fired the gun again and again into the man's body. Chamberlain ran out of the office and said to him, 'What's this you have done?' Richardson raised his arms and said to him, 'What I have done I can give myself up for.' He seemed to be quite passive as Chamberlain took him to the Westgate Police Station, where Police Constable Carr, Police Sergeant Haines and Inspector Gunn arrested him. Richardson made no attempt to escape and remained calm while he was searched and the gun found in his pocket. It was an ordinary six-chambered weapon, and four shots had been fired. After being arrested and searched, Richardon was then placed in a cell. Meanwhile, several people had collected around the injured William Burridge, who was still lying in the road. He was lifted into a nearby office and a doctor was sent for. Two doctors – Halton and Knowles – arrived within minutes, and the wounded man was quickly conveyed to the Beckett Hospital. At that point he was unconscious, but still breathing. He was examined by Dr Pye (house surgeon), Dr Halton and Dr Lancaster, who found that one bullet had entered his back near the spine, and another had entered his left temple. They made an attempt to remove the bullet in his head, but it had entered too far into the skull to be retrieved. Mrs Burridge

Westgate Police Station.

Borough Police Court.

visited him in the hospital, but found her husband unconscious and unable to recognize her.

The work of the Borough Police Court had concluded for the day but the mayor had not left, and so when he heard about the shooting and that Richardson was going to be brought into the magistrates' court, he remained where he was. The prisoner appeared before the mayor, Mr C. Brady, and Alderman Marsden on a charge of the attempted murder of William Burridge earlier that morning. Superintendent Kane attended and told the court what little he knew of the crime. The magistrate asked what the state of the victim was, and the superintendent stated that he was in a very precarious condition, and he was not expected to live much longer. The mayor suggested that a dying deposition was taken from the man, if he was capable of speech, and the prisoner was placed on remand. Superintendent Kane went to Richardson's house to search it. His wife admitted that she knew that he had a gun as he had owned it for several years. She told the superintendent that it was usually kept in a drawer at the house, but when he asked her to fetch it for him she found it had gone. She described how her husband had returned home that morning, but she did not see him load the gun or put it into his pocket. Mrs Richardson told him that her husband had not mentioned Burridge to her, but she had since found out that there had been some enmity between the two men for some time.

On Wednesday, 28 March 1888, James Richardson was again brought before the magistrates. His wife, sister and father were in court. They seemed much affected when Richardson was placed in the dock, but he remained cool and collected. It seems that William Burridge was still in a state of near death, which might result at any time, and another remand was granted. On the afternoon of Sunday, 1 April 1888, William Burridge died of his wounds at the Beckett Hospital. On Wednesday, 4 April, Richardson was again brought into court, this time charged with murder. Arthur Senior, the deceased man's brother-in-law, had identified the body. Evidence was given from Frank Chamberlain of how Richardson had repeatedly shot at Burridge while the injured man lay on the floor. The witness stated that when Burridge left the office, he saw Richardson through the

The single-storey building in the front of the picture is the only remains of Beckett Hospital today.

window and thought that he looked 'very excited'. An office boy, William Illingworth, also gave evidence of hearing the shots and seeing Burridge lying on the ground. Richardson was then remanded for another week.

On Wednesday, 4 April, an inquest was held for William Burridge at the Beckett Hospital before the coroner, Mr J. Taylor. Richardson's solicitor, Mr Rideal, watched the case for his client, who was not present. Surgeon Mr John Blackburn deposed to seeing the injured man many times, but he told the inquest that his patient was unable to speak and had never regained consciousness. A post-mortem had been carried out the previous day and Mr Blackburn had found one bullet embedded in the muscles of the deceased man's back. Another was in the right part of the upper hemisphere of the head. He stated that the cause of death was disintegration and irritation of the brain, followed by general exhaustion. The surgeon told the coroner that he had done everything he could have done for his patient, but he knew that nothing could have been done to prevent his death, which was inevitable. He expressed his opinion that it was a wonder that Burridge had lived so long after being shot in the head.

Frank Chamberlain said that after the shots he saw Richardson run away towards the entrance to the works on Dodworth Road. He ran after him and shouted at him to stop, and Richardson looked round and then, almost resignedly, walked slowly back towards him. Richardson then threw up both arms and gave himself up. The two men then calmly walked to the police station. On the way Richardson told Chamberlain that Burridge had sneered at him as he came out of Chamberlain's office. He added that for two years the foreman had been trying to ruin him. PC Carr stated that the two men had entered the police station at 12.10 pm on the day of the incident, and Richardson appeared to be very calm at the time. When he asked the prisoner for the gun he took it out of his pocket and handed it to him without a word. The coroner summed up for the jury, telling them not to worry about trying to find a motive for the crime. Their responsibility was simply to find James Richardson guilty or not of the death of William Burridge. The jury returned a verdict of wilful murder against James Richardson. On Friday,

6 April 1888, the funeral of William Burridge took place at Barnsley Cemetery in front of a large crowd of spectators. The coffin was described as being made of 'polished pitch pine with large brass handles'. The plate read: 'William Burridge, died April 1st 1888 aged 47 years'. The widow and her four children, along with other relatives and friends, walked in front of a large group of mourners and the burial service was read by The Reverend W.G. Hall, the Wesleyan minister.

On Thursday, 3 May, James Richardson was brought before the judge, Mr Justice Mathew, at Leeds Assizes. The prisoner appeared to be very abject as he stood in the dock, and during the hearing of the case, which lasted only two hours, he sat with his head buried in his hands. The prosecution, Mr Banks, opened the case and stated that there was no doubt that William Burridge had died from a bullet through the brain, and that Richardson had clearly been seen firing the weapon. He told the jury that in his opinion there could be no question but that Richardson had the gun on his person and therefore the murder was deliberately planned and wilfully carried out. As to the motive, it was obvious that the two men had been quarrelling. Several witnesses who were present at the shooting once again gave the same evidence as they had at the inquest. Arthur Bostick, another labourer at the firm, told the court that on the day of the shooting he heard the two men quarrelling, but was not close enough to hear what had been said.

At the conclusion of the case for the prosecution, Richardson's defence counsel asked the court for permission for the prisoner to make a statement, which was agreed. Richardson rose and in a quavering voice told the court that he had gone to work in his usual spirits. He hadn't been at work long when Burridge gave him his orders, and then the two men got into an argument about a brush that had been broken. Burridge claimed that Richardson had done it on purpose and when he tried to defend himself, Burridge then told him that he had better go home. When he asked for his wages, Burridge told him that Mr Frank Chamberlain would pay him later that morning. He went home and had breakfast and confessed to his wife that he 'had been finished', and she told him, 'Don't worry, lad, you will soon get another situation.' Far from the crime being premeditated, as the prosecution had stated, Richardson claimed that only after he left the house did he find the revolver in his pocket. Two days earlier he had been cleaning it in order to pawn it. He admitted that when he went for his wages and he noted the two men talking in the office, he saw Burridge look out of the window and deliberately put out his tongue at him. Richardson claimed that Burridge was laughing as he came out of the office, and that he elbowed him in the stomach as he passed. The prisoner told the court that at that moment:

> I felt a terrible feeling in my heart and I don't remember anything more until Mr Chamberlain said, 'Richardson what have you done?' Then I realized what I had done and saw poor Burridge on the ground and not withstanding my young wife and child, I would have given my life if I could have called him back.

Mr Justice Mathew asked Richardson how long he had had the gun, and he replied that he had bought the revolver on 5 November the previous year from a young man for about half a crown (two shillings and sixpence). His wife did not like having the gun on the premises, so it had been locked away for safety. He said that he hoped to pledge it in order to get some money for Easter, and then told the court, 'That is all I have to say.'

At the end of his long statement Richardson burst into tears as his defence, Mr Mellor, rose to address the court. Mellor stated that the prisoner had readily admitted that he had committed the offence. He pointed out that Richardson had not run away after the shooting but had given himself up. He stated that the fact that he had gone home and told his wife about the sacking, to which she had replied sympathetically, hardly indicated a rankling in his mind for revenge. Therefore, the assumption that the prisoner had taken the revolver to shoot at the deceased was negated by his statement. As his defence counsel he saw no reason to disbelieve him, but he asked the jury to bear in mind the provocation that he had suffered. Only when he thought he saw Burridge laughing at him, did he take out the gun and shoot him. There was no premeditation and when Richardson saw what he had done, and he was immediately sorry for his actions. Mr Justice Mathew summed up and questioned why Richardson had not made this statement earlier, but the prisoner made no reply. The judge told the jury that they had to decide whether the murder was a deliberate act or not on the part of the prisoner. The statement that the prisoner had made was to suggest that it was not a deliberate act, but due to sudden provocation. However, His Lordship stated that there did not appear to him to be any reason in his statement to reduce the charge from murder to manslaughter.

The jury retired to consider their verdict. After an absence of only twenty minutes they returned with a verdict of guilty, but they asked for a recommendation for mercy. The judge put on the black cap and, addressing the prisoner, told him:

> Richardson, the jury could have pronounced no other verdict than the one they have given against you with any regard to their oaths. It is no part of my duty to add to the misery of your position with words of reproach for the crime of which you have been convicted. So far as the evidence shows, you sent a perfectly inoffensive man out of this world, without notice, and you must be prepared to be punished.

Richardson was then sentenced to death. He was weeping so much that he had to be supported by two warders as he was removed from the dock. Soon after his sentence he wrote to his wife from his prison cell at Armley Gaol. According to a newspaper report, he thanked her for her support and asked her to tell their daughter when she grew up, that 'her father died a victim to his own passionate temper'. He asked her to come and visit him when she could, signing it from 'her loving, but unfortunate husband James William Richardson'. It was announced on 16 May that the executions of Richardson, Dr Burke (see Chapter Thirteen) and a woman who had been sentenced to death for the murder of her child would take place on 22 May 1888.

Petitions were being gathered by the condemned men's solicitors and Richardson must have felt some hope when it was announced on Monday, 21 May that the woman's and Dr Burke's sentences were to be respited. Many of the jurors that had been involved in Richardson's case had written to the Home Secretary asking that he be reprieved. It was reported that more than 7,000 signatures from working-class people of South Yorkshire had also been sent to London. So there was a positive outcry when it was realized that Richardson would be the only one of the three condemned prisoners to be executed. Back in Barnsley that same day, a town crier went round the town, ringing his bell and announcing to the people of Barnsley that a public meeting was to be held at noon in Peel Square to protest at the decision. In response, nearly 3,000 people attended, including Richardson's father and his solicitor, Mr Rideal. The solicitor announced that the people of the town were dissatisfied with the decision that James Richardson was the only one of the three condemned not to receive a reprieve. He suggested that a telegram be sent to Queen Victoria from the people of Barnsley begging that the condemned man's life be spared.

Realizing that there was little time left, a man called Mr Patterson was dispatched to deliver the petition in person to London, and he left on the 2.00 pm train. Sadly, Mr Rideal received a telegram later that night saying that the Secretary of State had examined the case again, but was 'unable to interfere with the course of justice'. Despite the late hour, at 10.00 pm another public meeting was held in Peel Square, attended this time by 6,000 people. The telegram was read out and many people expressed the feeling that a great injustice was being done. Anger was articulated as the fact that at Richardson's trial the jury had asked for leniency, which had been ignored. It was pointed out that no such appeal had been made in the case of Dr Burke, yet his sentence had been commuted. Once again, telegrams were sent to the Home Office bearing the signature of the mayor of Barnsley and other prominent citizens of the town, praying for a stay of execution for James William Richardson.

On the morning of the execution Richardson awoke after passing a good night's rest. On the previous day he had written to his father and mother, and another letter to his wife and child. He also gave the governor, Mr Green, several small articles such as books and other items that had been lent to him by sympathizers. He requested that after his death they be forwarded to his relatives. That morning he was pinioned in his cell shortly before 8.00 am by the executioner, Billington, and a procession was formed to walk to the scaffold, which was only about 20 yards away from the cell of the condemned. Richardson, walking between two lines of warders, showed no emotion as he crossed the yard. The prisoner was swiftly placed on the trap door and, at a given signal, Billington drew the bolt and Richardson fell into the pit, appearing to die without a struggle. A crowd of people had assembled outside the prison gates to witness the raising of the black flag to indicate that the execution had taken place.

Irrespective of the fact that the execution could no longer be halted, anger and hostility towards the Home Secretary continued to bubble in Barnsley. The following week, on Monday, 28 May, another protest meeting was held in Monk Bretton, where people attended from Cudworth, Carlton, Smithies and all the surrounding villages. Even though Dr Burke had lived at Monk Bretton, the meeting was to protest at his reprieve

The tower at Armley Gaol, where the bodies of executed prisoners were removed for burial.

and the fact that Richardson had been executed. The meeting was arranged in order that 'the neighbourhood now assembled, strongly and emphatically protests against the actions of the Home Secretary'. They complained that he had ignored the recommendations of the jury in the case of James Richardson and yet he had advised Her Majesty to respite the sentence of Dr Burke, 'and that the prerogative of mercy was more suitable to Richardson rather than Dr Burke'. The meeting requested that an enquiry be made into the matter and that questions be asked in Parliament by the local MP, Mr C.S. Kenny, about the decision made by the Home Secretary. The proposition was carried unanimously, and it was agreed that it be sent to Mr Kenny in Parliament and to Prime Minister Lord Salisbury.

It was a long time before the people of Barnsley forgot the actions of the Home Secretary and the injustice of the execution of James Richardson. The condemnation of the system of capital punishment was heard once again in national newspapers, and discussions took place as to whether it was relevant at all in a modern, civilized society. Other methods of execution were proposed and more humane means of carrying them out argued for, but it was all too late for the wife and relatives of James Richardson.

CHAPTER FIFTEEN

Saved by her Stays

In some crimes there is a very fine dividing line between murder and attempted murder. Some cases would have resulted in murder if not for the lucky intervention of fate. In this case, the 'lucky intervention' was the strength of a woman's stays, or corsets. In the nineteenth century, many fashionable young women chose to wear corsets in an attempt to narrow their waists and present an hourglass figure. This was achieved by the insertion of steel or bone strips in the corset material. Although corsets were later criticized for practically deforming women's inner organs, this woman had reason to thank providence that she was wearing a garment that ended up saving her life.

In December 1888, Charles Williams was a 22-year-old unemployed collier who was involved with a young woman called Mary Sarah Phillips. The couple had cohabited together as man and wife for about four years as they lived in various towns and villages in Yorkshire and Derbyshire. They went from one place to another, never staying in one area for very long. They had to keep a low profile because Williams was not only a very disreputable character, but was also a deserter from the Army. Three years previously, a child had been born to the couple and for a short while they settled down at Chapeltown, Sheffield. But this stability was not to last as Williams had a history of violence. On 7 December 1888, they argued once more, and agreed to separate. Mary Phillips and the child went to live with her parents in Barnsley at their house on Thomas Street, whilst Williams stayed in Sheffield. On several occasions he visited her at her parents' home and begged her to come back to live with him again, but she always refused.

Mary didn't see Williams again until 19 December, when she met him near Thomas Street. She was carrying the child in her arms when Williams seized the baby and took it away from her.

Thomas Street.

Mary pleaded with him to give the child back to her, and he said that he would if she would come and live with him again. Mary refused to do so and he walked away with the baby. Before he left he threatened her, saying that because he was a deserter if she told anyone where he was, he would 'knife her'. His continual threats and ill treatment of her when they were together preyed on Mary's mind, and she was convinced he would end up murdering her. So, on the morning of Saturday, 29 December, when Mary received a letter from Williams stating that her child was ill with bronchitis, she grew very afraid. He said that he wished her to meet him at the gates of Locke Park, Barnsley, at 7.00 pm that night. But Mary felt this was just a ruse to get her to a place that would be isolated so she burned the letter and refused to meet him. At 10.20 pm, she was visiting her brother at his house on Burleigh Street, where she met a young man called Thomas Siddons, who was a miner. Knowing that she was afraid of Williams still, her brother asked Siddons if he would escort his sister home. The young man agreed and Mary left the house in company with him. They talked amicably to each other as they walked along the street.

Unbeknownst to Mary, Williams had secreted himself in a nearby public house and had been watching the house. Looking

The gates of Locke Park.

Burleigh Street as it is today.

out of the window, he saw her walking along with a young man and he was infuriated. He crept up behind the young couple and suddenly Mary was viciously struck from behind by some object, and was instantly felled to the ground. Williams fell on top of her, and in front of her young companion stabbed at her again and again. Thankfully, the blows to Mary's chest were deflected by the steel in her stays, which broke the blade in Williams' hand. Before her companion could act, an unnamed young woman who had seen the attack struck Williams over the back of his head with an umbrella that she was carrying. Getting to his feet, Williams immediately ran off. Medical help was called for and Dr John Blackburn, the police surgeon, attended. He found that Mary had been stabbed more than eight times in various parts of her body. She also had many defence wounds on her arms and hands, sustained as she had struggled with her assailant to try to prevent further injury to herself. It was afterwards suggested that if this woman had not attacked him with her umbrella, Williams would have completed his purpose and killed Mary Phillips.

Mary was able to give the name of her attacker and a search was made for Charles Williams. He was arrested at a public house in Barnsley by Police Constable Fisher. What Mary did not know was that, earlier that night, Williams had gone to a public house called the Marquis of Granby Inn, which was near to where she lived with her parents. He spoke to a young man called John Firth, whom he had known when he worked as a collier. It was reported that, as the two men stood in the yard at the back of the public house, Williams said that 'he would tell Firth something if he didn't tell anyone else'. He then showed him a pocket knife that he carried, and said that he intended to murder Mary Phillips that very night.

On Monday, 31 December 1888, Charles Williams was brought before magistrates Mr J. Dyson, Mr H. Piggott and Mr T. Dymond at the Barnsley Court House. He was charged with cutting and wounding with intent to do grievous bodily harm. Williams told the magistrate that he had no fixed abode. When asked how he pleaded, he told the clerk that he was innocent of carrying out the attack. Mary Sarah Phillips was the first witness, and she described the events leading up to the attack on her. John Firth confirmed his conversation with Williams in the Marquis of Granby public house. He stated that he was so horrified at what the prisoner had told him that he had dreamed about the incident for a fortnight afterwards. Dr Blackburn stated that he had examined the woman soon after the attack and had found many wounds on her. He said that she had two small incised wounds on the right temple, two others on the forehead, three small wounds on the right side of her nose, one wound on the upper lip, one wound on the wrist that measured about half an inch and a smaller wound on her little finger. He said that, in his opinion, the wounds were caused by the knife he had been shown, which had belonged to the prisoner.

The knife that had been used in the attack was then shown to the magistrates. It was described as 'an evil looking weapon'. PC Fisher stated that when he arrested Williams on the charge of attempted murder, he had said to him, 'That's all right; I hope the beggar is dead.' PC Fisher said that even when he was in custody, the prisoner frequently stated that he wished that Mary Phillips had died. Apart from admitting that he had no fixed abode and was innocent, Williams did not speak during the whole time that the court was in session. The magistrates

Sheffield Town Hall.

found him guilty, and he was sent to take his trial at the West Riding Quarter Sessions at Sheffield Town Hall.

He was brought to Sheffield at the adjourned Christmas sessions, which were held on Friday, 4 January 1889. Colonel Stanhope CB presided, and the other justices of the peace on the bench were Colonel Neville, Mr T.H. Jeffcock, Mr J. Kaye and Mr Dyson. Colonel Stanhope, as the chair, addressed the jury before the trial started. He drew the court's attention to all of the cases before them, three of which were for wounding with knives. He stated that there was an increase in these sorts of crimes, and he was determined to deal with the culprits severely. Colonel Stanhope pointed out that these cases were more serious than thefts of property, and the prisoners would be sentenced accordingly. The first case of stabbing was that of a son who had stabbed his mother, but being her mainstay of support she was reluctant to give evidence against him and he was found not guilty and discharged.

As Charles Williams was the second prisoner to be brought into the courtroom on the charge of wounding, and he pleaded guilty to wounding Mary Phillips, he had high hopes that he too would be discharged. The prosecution was Mr Waddy and the prisoner was defended by Mr Ellis. Mr Waddy outlined the case for the jury, and several witnesses gave evidence to what was referred to as 'a most brutal assault'. However, the bench stated that this case was a particularly bad one due to the level of violence inflicted and the premeditation involved in the crime. Nevertheless, Williams was so convinced that he would get off that when the magistrates found him guilty and sentenced him to five years' imprisonment, he fainted in the dock. The third case of stabbing heard that day also resulted in the attacker being found not guilty, and that prisoner too was discharged. Williams must have pondered on the fickleness of fate, which had left him the only one to be found guilty out of the three cases of wounding. The reality was that he had sealed his own fate when he boasted about the attack beforehand, and it was this that had actually condemned him.

CHAPTER SIXTEEN

A Brutal Attack on an Elderly Landlady

Another brutal attack, which was made on a 68-year-old widow called Mrs Rebecca Lawrence, took place in January of 1893 at her house at Lister's Buildings, Great Houghton, about 6 miles from Barnsley. Mrs Lawrence was supported by both her sons, who lived with her and worked as miners at the Houghton Main Colliery. Strangely to our modern ears, Mrs Lawrence and her two sons slept in the same room, and she let the other rooms out as lodgings. On the evening of Sunday, 29 January 1893, she was already in bed when she saw her son William take out his purse and lay out some coins, which amounted to £11. Taking off his clothes he placed the money into a box, which was on a table at the side of the bed. He locked the box and put the key under his mattress. At 4.00 am the next morning Mrs Lawrence called her two sons out of their beds in time for work. Both were due at work at 5.30 am that morning. The young men dressed in the dark and left for work, leaving their mother alone in bed at the house. William set out for work at 5.00 am, and Richard left the house about a quarter of an hour later. About ten minutes or so after they had gone, Mrs Lawrence heard a window being pushed up and the sound of her son's dog, a fox terrier, begin to bark in the kitchen. Thinking it was Richard who had forgotten something and returned, she called out to him, 'Dick, is that you?' but got no answer, and the dog continued to bark.

She was not particularly disturbed and remained in bed as she thought that Richard perhaps hadn't heard her call out. Presently, Mrs Lawrence heard someone coming up the stairs, but she was curious because they made no sound, as if they had taken their shoes off. Just then a man came into her bedroom. He was crouched over, with his face hidden. Still assuming it was her son, she said, 'Dick, you frightened me.

Why did you not call out?' With that the man straightened up and hit the elderly woman savagely across the head with a poker that she kept in the kitchen, causing blood to flow freely down her face. Not a word was spoken during the attack. The man then put a hand over her nose and mouth, and seized her around the throat until she blacked out. When Mrs Lawrence came to, the room was empty and the sheets on her bed were all covered in blood. Just then the same man came back into the room, and as he approached the window, where it was lighter, she got a good look at his face. She recognized him as her former lodger, a man called Harry Hodgson, who was aged about twenty-four and was married with one child. Mrs Lawrence was also convinced that someone else was in the house with Hodgson as an accomplice. Although the elderly woman didn't see anyone else, she thought that she heard someone else moving about.

Mrs Lawrence showed remarkable coolness as she saw Hodgson approach the bed again. He put his ear near to her cheek to test if she was still breathing. Mrs Lawrence remained as still as she could, and held her breath. The burglar then went to William's bed and removed the key from under the mattress where it was always kept and opened his box. Hodgson took the money and then went downstairs. Shortly after her ordeal the aged woman managed to get to the house of her neighbour, a woman called Mrs Rebecca Blaney. After Mrs Lawrence related her story to her neighbour, Mrs Blaney raised the alarm and called for a constable. Surgeon Mr Richard Castle was called and he attended to the stricken woman. Police Constable Marples, who was stationed at Great Houghton, was dispatched to the scene and he took Mrs Lawrence's statement. He looked around the house and found that Hodgson and his possible accomplice had gained access to the house by unfastening a latch on one of the ground-floor windows. He also noted that although the robbers had taken £11 in change from the box in the bedroom, they missed other coins amounting to another £10, which were hidden beneath some papers. Mrs Lawrence told PC Marples that one of the coins had been a sixpence and was very distinctive as it was a jubilee coin. Her son William had a hole drilled in it, with the intention of having it as an ornament on his watch chain. PC Marples then arrested Harry Hodgson at his lodgings in Kitson's Row, Great Houghton.

It was reported that Hodgson had previously lodged with Mrs Lawrence and her two sons from March to December 1892, when for some unknown reason he was asked to leave. So there was little doubt that during that time he lodged at the house he would have been very well acquainted with the layout and would have easily observed the places where money was kept. Mrs Lawrence had told PC Marples that the burglar had known exactly where to find the money and had gone straight for it. Later that same morning, Harry Hodgson appeared in the courtroom in Barnsley in front of magistrates Messrs T. Brady and T. Dymond. The prisoner was charged with breaking and entering the dwelling house of Mrs Rebecca Lawrence earlier that day, as well as her attempted murder. Superintendent Kane described how, in the course of the burglary, Hodgson had ferociously attacked his former landlady over the head with a poker. The superintendent stated that since the attack Mrs Lawrence was in a very precarious state of health. Consequently, he asked for the prisoner to be remanded until the following Friday. The surgeon, Mr Castle, gave evidence that he found the patient suffering from serious wounds on her head. He gave his opinion that they were caused by a poker, or some such implement, and one of the wounds had penetrated down to the bone. When he examined Mrs Lawrence he found that she was suffering from a great loss of blood, and that although she was still very unwell he did not at that time consider her to be in any danger. The magistrates remanded the prisoner once more.

On 10 February 1893, Harry Hodgson was once again brought into court, where he immediately spotted his former landlady. The magistrates on this occasion were Messrs C. Harvey and C.H. Taylor. Mr W.E. Raley outlined the case for the prosecution and the first witness was Mrs Lawrence herself. The old woman looked extremely frail, and was clearly still in a very delicate state of health as she gave her evidence from a seat in the courtroom. The elderly woman had a large bandage wrapped around her head, and courageously described the night of the attack. She stated that a few weeks previously, while the prisoner had been lodging at her house, she had complained about the faulty catch on the front downstairs window.

PC Marples told the court how he had apprehended the prisoner at his house on 30 January. He told the magistrates that when the house was searched, he found the stolen coins, including the sixpence that had been drilled in the middle. The constable had also found a blue and white striped jersey, the collar of which had been smeared with blood. He deduced that the blood was that of Mrs Lawrence, and was thought to have been smeared onto Hodgson's collar as he leant over the body after the attack to see if she was breathing. PC Marples described how he had taken the prisoner to the cells at Westgate Police Station at Barnsley, and there he charged him with breaking into the house at some time between 5.00 am and 6.00 am that morning. The prisoner denied the charge and stated that he had not been out of the house since the previous evening. PC Marples told the court how he later returned to the victim's house and examined the broken sash window. The top sash had been pulled right down, and there was an amount of mud on the inside of the window sill as well as on the sofa that stood beneath. William Lawrence was the next to give evidence and he corroborated much of his mother's story, and also identified the sixpence as being his own.

The cells to the rear of Westgate Police Station.

Sergeant Taylor told the magistrates that he was stationed at Wombwell, and that he had accompanied PC Marples to the elderly woman's home just after she had been attacked. He described how he had found the poker still covered in blood; it had been placed at the foot of the bed in which Mrs Lawrence normally slept. Sergeant Taylor had also gone to the prisoner's house on the same day and had helped the constable to search the property. Taylor described finding the stolen money in an ornament on the prisoner's mantleshelf. He also described seeing the marks of blood on the right side of the striped jersey. At this point the magistrates asked Hodgson if he had anything to say and he replied that he hadn't. The magistrates told him that for the charge of breaking and entering the property, he would be sent to take his trial at the next assizes. He then went into the case of the attempted murder of Mrs Lawrence on the morning of 30 January. Mrs Lawrence then described the events of the early morning attack and stated that she distinctly saw the prisoner enter her bedroom by moonlight and attack her. Her neighbour, Rebecca Blaney, described how the injured woman had come to her house that morning with her forehead bleeding profusely. The magistrates informed the prisoner that he had been found guilty and was committed to take his trial for attempted murder.

Hodgson appeared at Leeds Town Hall in front of Justice Bruce on Thursday, 16 March 1893. He was sentenced to five years' penal servitude – a very light sentence for a man who might so easily have been charged with a most brutal murder.

CHAPTER SEVENTEEN

The Second Monk Bretton Mystery

After the sensational murder by Dr Burke, Monk Bretton returned to being the quiet little backwater village it had been previously. So it was with some concern that the people of the village learned of another murder a few years later. On Sunday, 2 April 1899, the body of a 63-year-old woman was discovered in a disued quarry, which was situated just off Cliffe Lane. The woman lay on the approach to the quarry, visible through a stone archway. At about 9.00 am, miner Samuel Cooper was on his way to work when he found the body lying on the ground. Next to it was the woman's hat, shawl and umbrella. Her head was almost under the archway, and only the lower part of her body and legs could be seen from the road itself. The police were called and the body was removed to the Norman Inn. The police surgeon, Dr Sweeney, was called and on examining the body he found several fingermarks around the neck, which proved that the woman had been strangled. Her dress had been torn in the struggle and the pockets were cut away, which suggested that robbery had been the motive.

Superintendent Kane, Detective Sergeant Etherington and Sergeant Grundy were quickly on the scene. They found that the woman was a widow named Ann Whitehead, of Albert Street, Barnsley, and she had last been seen in the Norman Inn on the previous afternoon. She had known the area around Monk Bretton well as she had previously lived there at a house on Castle Street, only a stone's throw from where her body was found. It seems that Ann had gone into the inn and asked the landlord, Marmaduke Pickles Herbert, for a drink. Noticing that she was already 'under the influence', he refused to serve her, and she left around 1.00 pm. Enquiries found that previous to her visit to the public house Ann had been seen at the Sun Inn, where the landlady had similarly refused to serve her. It was noted that at that time she had 4s 2d in her purse. Neither

Albert Street.

the money nor the purse was found on the body. It was known that Ann had acted as a housekeeper for a man in the locality until about six or eight weeks previously, but even in that short period, she had changed her address several times. Police enquiries quickly established that she had last been seen in the company of a 25-year-old man called Richard Wormald, and on the Sunday night he was arrested.

An inquest was held for Ann Whitehead at the Norman Inn on Monday, 3 April before the coroner, Mr P.P. Maitland. Attending the inquest was the prisoner, who was stated as being from Monk Bretton and had been taken before the magistrates at Barnsley earlier that morning. Superintendent Kane said that after the deceased had been refused a drink at the Sun Inn, she was put out of the house by the landlord's wife and a woman called Mrs Vickers. Ann then went to the Norman Inn, where she saw Wormald standing at the other side of the bar and went over and spoke to him. A miner from Littleworth, Alfred Scales told the inquest that he saw the man he knew as Richard Thomas Wormald entering the Norman Inn the previous night. He had only been there a short while before Ann Whitehead entered. Scales stated that Wormald greeted the deceased woman in a way that did not seem to be prearranged. They had a few drinks together before she told him that she had business at Littleworth, and Wormald agreed to accompany her. The couple continued their conversation as they walked out of the pub and headed in the direction of the disused quarry, where the body was later to be found. PC Grundy stated that after Wormald had been cautioned, he said, 'I know nothing whatever about it.' The prisoner told him that he had seen Ann Whitehead on the Saturday night and had seen her leave the public house, but that he had remained behind for another three minutes before walking through Cross Street to another part of the village. Wormald was asked if he met anyone after leaving the inn, but stated that he had not. Samuel Cooper gave evidence on finding the body, and Dr Sweeney gave his evidence to say that one of the bones in the deceased woman's throat had been fractured during the strangulation. The coroner summed up for the jury, stating that if they were satisfied that there was a presumptive case against any person, to return a verdict against that person. The jury took little time to return, giving a verdict that the woman had been murdered 'by person or persons unknown'. Despite the jury's findings the coroner ordered that Richard Wormald was to be remanded in custody until further enquires could be made.

On Friday, 7 April, Wormald was once again brought into court. Mr Carrington prosecuted the case on behalf of the Treasury, stating that he had not had time to study the case and asked for a further remand, which was agreed. Mr Rideal, Wormald's defence solicitor, requested an early hearing, pointing out that the verdict of the inquest jury 'had practically taken his client out of the case'. Therefore, he asked for an early opportunity to clear his client's name. It was agreed that Wormald would be remanded until Monday next. On 1 April the prisoner was again in court, before several magistrates, but on this occasion there was no jury. Once more he protested his innocence and denied meeting Ann Whitehead after she left the Norman Inn. Despite the defence solicitor's conviction of the innocence of his client, the magistrates did not agree. Even though the evidence, which was much the same as it had been presented at the inquest, was repeated, the magistrates decided that the inquest jury was wrong. Richard Wormald was found guilty and committed to taking his trial.

However, before he could appear at the Leeds Assizes on Tuesday, 9 May 1899, as was usual, the grand jury assessed the cases before them. The judge, Mr Justice Hucknall, commented on the fact that the only real evidence against Richard Wormald was the fact that he had been the last person to be seen in the woman's company before she was found dead. He told them that the couple had been seen outside the Norman Inn talking together, and the conversation seemed to be of a friendly nature. No one saw any quarrel, or any act that would lead them to believe that the pair had quarreled. The next morning the woman's body was found a mile and a half from the inn, and that was all the evidence against the man so far as he could see. He added before the grand jury could send this man down to be tried for his life, they would have to be very satisfied that there was a *prima facie* case against him. Concluding that he would not presume to dictate to the grand jury, but unless they saw more in the depositions than he had, it would be hard to send the man to be tried for his life on those few details. On the following day Wormald was brought up from the cells and into the courtroom. Mr Justice Hucknall addressed Wormald and he told him:

> It was a matter of surprise that you had been committed for trial at all. So far as I am concerned I don't think there is a proper charge against you. You can go away absolutely without a spot on your character.

Wormald looked very relieved as he left the dock. But that was far from the end of the case.

On Tuesday, 2 January 1900, the body of Richard Thomas Wormald was found drowned. Following the assizes he had returned back to Monk Bretton, where he lived with his uncle and aunt, and had taken up his former employment. On 29 November, Wormald disappeared, and the following day a

The steps up to the dock at Leeds Assizes.

young man's cap was found floating in the Barnsley Canal at Cliffe Bridge. Extensive inquiries were made but nothing was heard until the body resurfaced. It was taken to the nearby Hope Inn, where it seems he had spent his last hours. An inquest was held by the coroner at the Sun Inn, Monk Bretton, where the body was identified by his uncle, Mr John Beaumont. He stated that the body had been searched and that he had identified his nephew's body by a club card with his name on that had been found in the dead man's pocket. Five weeks earlier, Mr Beaumont had also identified the cap that had been found in the canal as his nephew's. Mr Beaumont told the coroner that the deceased man had lived with him since he was fourteen years of age. He had taken in what he described as 'a poor helpless lad' when Wormald had gone to him of his own accord. He stated that he had had a row with his father, Mr Beaumont's brother, telling him that 'his father had never been a father to him at all'. The last time he had seen his nephew was five weeks previously, when he had been 'a strong, healthy young fellow' who had gone with the landlord of the Hope Inn to buy some pigs.

The coroner, Mr P.P. Maitland, asked him if the deceased had had any worries before he died and he replied, 'Only about that affair,' which the coroner took to mean the accusation of murder. Mr Beaumont stated:

> It never seemed to put him about. When he was at home I never saw any difference in him. Only in the last three weeks or a month he seemed more steady and more careful, and kept better hours. I thought he would turn over and be a right good lad again.

The coroner asked Mr Beaumont if his nephew had shown any signs of depression, but the witness told him that he hadn't and that he had seen no signs that he intended to take his own life. He added that there had been no suicide note in his pocket or anywhere else when he was found. Alfred North Wiseman stated that he was the landlord of the Hope Inn and that he knew the deceased well, as he had often come to the inn. On 28 November, Wormald went with him to Pontefract market, and on his return had stayed at the inn until after 10.30 pm. Mr Wiseman stated that Wormald was sober when he left by the back door, as was his usual custom. Wiseman had stood at the door and watched Wormald walk along the canal towpath. The coroner asked him if he had heard the deceased say anything about 'being tired of living', or any such other remarks. The witness told him that he had heard rumours that he had said something about it to others, but that he had never intimated as much to him. He was asked if Wormald had ever mentioned the murder case to him, and he told that they had never discussed it at all.

A boatman gave evidence of finding the body, and a woman named Ann Peaker stated that she had laid out the body and there were no signs of violence on it. The jury returned a verdict of 'found drowned without any marks of violence'. There is little evidence as to whether Richard Wormald was indeed guilty of the murder of Ann Whitehead, and less evidence for any motive. But the fact that he killed himself only seven months later suggests strongly that he was. His uncle could not account for his suicide, although he admitted that he had spoken about it to others. But if he was innocent, as he claimed, then the question remains as to who was the killer of Ann Whitehead.

Sources

Newspapers

Bradford Observer, The
Bristol Mercury
Daily Gazette, The
Daily News
Freeman's Journal, The
Huddersfield Chronicle
Hull Packet
Illustrated Police News
Leeds Mercury, The

Lloyds Illustrated News
Morning Chronicle, The
Morning Post, The
Northern Echo, The
Penny Illustrated Paper, The
Sheffield and Rotherham
    Independent
Standard, The
York Herald

Illustrations

Most are from the author's own collection, with the exception of:

Page 37:   Wortley Hall.
Page 53:   Row of houses at Smithies.
Page 98:   New Oaks Colliery.
Page 106:   Norman Inn, Monk Bretton.
Page 108:   Beckett Hospital.

All of the above were published by kind permission of Barnsley Archives and Local Studies.

Books

The Goaler's Journal and the Chaplain's Book, courtesy of York Museums Trust (York Castle Prison).

Index